Praise for *The Truth About Innovation*

"If you want to lead innovation eff[...]
everyone so that they all understa[...]
culture."
Dr. David Gillen, Innovati[...] [...]zer

"For once a book about innovation th[...] [...]t sound idealistic or
impractical. Max fills his text with great examples and simple 'rules'
which bring the subject to life, and at the same time show how innovation is possible anywhere, anytime."
Linda Holbeche, Research and Policy Director, CIPD

"Max's truths will expand what your company imagines to be possible
through the power of 'beautiful ideas' now and in the future."
Bryan Kirschner, Director of Open Source Strategy, Microsoft

"We now live in the Innovation Age. I loved this book – it will help you
begin and continue your lifelong innovation journey."
David Keene, VP Marketing and Competition, SAP

"Refreshingly helpful and stylishly entertaining: Max gives useful information which is excitingly new and common sense. This takes talent –
something he amply demonstrates in this thought-provoking book."
Professor David Crowther, De Montfort University

"It's a great book that shows innovation is about keeping our eyes and
minds open, questioning what we know and reconciling the irreconcilable. To keep at hand and share widely."
Helene Finidori, author of *The Menemani Blog*

"Max has created something of use to both new and experienced prac-
titioners. The bite-sized essay format is an easy read, and highly
recommended for anyone that wants to get a handle quickly on the
business – and process – of innovation."
Dr. James Gardner, Head of Innovation at Global Retail Bank

"The Truth About Innovation *is a highly provocative and engaging book
about the simple, yet often overlooked, important, yet often ignored, and
critical, yet often underestimated, rules of innovation. Pick up a copy!"*
Kevin C. Desouza, Director of Institute for Innovation, University of
Washington

"Most books on innovation are long-winded and vague, or thick and theoretical. Max has avoided these traps and written a book that's short, sharp and practical."

Alain Thys, Managing Partner of Futurelab, Curator of blog.futurelab.net

"Are companies ready for Max's message? More now than ever. He shows how ideas don't stand alone, how many companies are trapped in a vicious cycle of mimicry, and uses examples to explain how to jumpstart innovation."

Frances Legge, Sears Canada

"With his honest and down-to-earth style, Max has given us a book that will serve to break taboos and old habits in innovation. He has done what has been not been done before: a down-to-the-earth, no-phd-required guide to innovation."

Laurent Uhres, Founder of Yourthinktank.org

"Mckeown, in his usual forthright, informative, witty and highly readable way, invites us all to take a new look at innovation – and shows us why. This isn't about new for old – it's about new from old."

Jonathan Donovan, Townhouse Consulting and Ex Head of O2 Employee Relations

"If an intelligent, easy-to-follow, practical, and useful guide to innovation, growth, and change management is what you seek; your search ends here! I'll be buying this book for everyone on my team. Just brilliant!"

Rahim Dawood, Solutions Architect, dot2beyond Inc.

"As an innovation practitioner, there's true value in this book. It's extremely informative, with great examples and brief enough to keep your attention."

Paul R. Williams, CEO, Think For A Change

"Perceptive analysis of what works and what doesn't, with useful illustrations from real businesses. Thought-provoking, grounded and realistic."

Professor Khalid Aziz, The Aziz Corporation

THE TRUTH ABOUT

INNOVATION

Max Mckeown

Harlow, England • London • New York • Boston • San Francisco • Toronto
Sydney • Tokyo • Singapore • Hong Kong • Seoul • Taipei • New Delhi
Cape Town • Madrid • Mexico City • Amsterdam • Munich • Paris • Milan

PEARSON EDUCATION LIMITED

Edinburgh Gate
Harlow CM20 2JE
Tel: +44 (0)1279 623623
Fax: +44 (0)1279 431059
Website: www.pearsoned.co.uk

First published in Great Britain in 2008

© Pearson Education Limited 2008

ISBN: 978-0-273-71912-0

British Library Cataloguing-in-Publication Data
A catalogue record for this book is available from the British Library

Library of Congress Cataloging-in-Publication Data
McKeown, Max.
    The truth about innovation / Max Mckeown.
       p. cm.
    Includes bibliographical references.
    ISBN 978-0-273-71912-0 (pbk.)
    1. Organizational change. 2. Organizational effectiveness. I. Title.
    HD58.8.M3468 2008
    658.4'063–dc22

                          2008029808

10 9 8 7 6 5 4 3 2 1
12 11 10 09 08

Typeset in 10/13 pt Meta-LightLF by 3
Printed and bound in Great Britain by Ashford Colour Press Ltd, Gosport

The publisher's policy is to use paper manufactured from sustainable forests.

Innovation rocks. It rolls. It makes the world go round. Our lifestyles are the result of other people's efforts to improve the human condition. They mixed ideas and inventions together. They worked hard to create the must-have and often taken-for-granted stuff that surrounds us.

You have evolution to thank for your opposable thumbs and adorable belly button. And for your amazing brain, with more connections than stars in the galaxy, that has allowed millions and now billions of us to examine our world and seek to make it better. That is innovation and it matters.

Innovation is a fad. It's a fashion. At least that's what cynics will say after a few years of talking about its importance. After the innovation boom will come the innovation bust. The smart companies will keep innovating and the wannabes will stop. Smart people know the difference between fashion and fact.

Our century's greatest innovation will be the method of innovation. We are beginning to understand how to increase our ability to improve together. We are learning how to move from individual invention to group innovation.

This book shares some of what we have learned about innovation, what it is, how it happens, and how you can increase it. New insights into how our brains work collectively provide us with the opportunity to create the equivalent of a bigger brain, capable of dreaming and working together to make those dreams reality.

If you want to make your world better, this book is worth your time. If you have been working with innovation for years, this work will remind you of what you know and still give you new insights. If you want to help colleagues to understand what it takes to move from ideas to insights to innovation, then this is the book that you should buy for them.

Everyone can help. Every kind of intelligence and personality plays a part. Our need for innovation has shifted power closer to the source of that power—Us. We are the future.

TRUTH

1

Innovation is new stuff that is made useful

Innovation is new stuff that is made useful. That's just about the best definition. It clears up what's interesting about innovation without overcomplicating. It also leads to the two questions that you should be asking next: Useful for whom? How new is new?

Usefulness is in the eye of the user. If you have an idea for improving something but do nothing with it—then you have not invented or innovated. If you don't share it you haven't even helped anyone else to invent or innovate—the idea will die with you. If you share your idea then it becomes an insight. If you put your insight into practice, it becomes an invention. If your invention is useful to someone then the invention has become an innovation. If the innovation increases human happiness then perhaps we have made progress.

People invent solutions for themselves because they can't find, can't afford or won't buy an off-the-shelf product that meets their need.

Usefulness is in the eye of the user.

The greater the need the greater the incentive to invent. People invent solutions for other people because they have recognised the need. Inventing useful things for people that they are willing to buy is the basis of commerce and economic prosperity.

Newness is also judged by the user. An idea you have never heard of is new to you. An idea your colleagues have never heard of or never used is new to your company. Two old ideas mixed together are new and may be new enough to be useful in different ways that are useful to someone. Even better, they may be useful enough to give you something you value in exchange. Swapping stuff that is accepted and perfected in one country but appears new and difficult to do in another country is the basis of international trade. Some of what we used to swap was raw materials that just happened to be in one country rather than another but increasingly what we swap is rich with ideas, insights and innovation.

People may not want something to be completely new. An invention can be so new that it doesn't fit into anyone's life. They may reject an idea because it challenges their way of looking at the world. Or because it is simply too much work to change the way they have always worked.

People may not want something to be completely new.

All innovations are new; however, they vary in their degree of newness:

- **Incremental** innovation involves small steps, something that is a minor improvement to an existing solution. Small steps have taken Gillette from one razor blade, to two, three and now five blades.
- **Radical** innovations take big steps, creating major improvements that are often very different from existing solutions. Cloning "Dolly" the sheep qualifies as a radical innovation—it was a first and it was certainly a breakthrough.
- **Revolutions** happen when groups of these innovations can together cause a huge, far-reaching impact. The computing revolution was achieved because of thousands of new technologies, including the microprocessor, the telephone and the television. Globalisation, the Human Genome Project and the Lunar Landing would not have been possible without it.

In reality, these innovations often rely on each other. Incremental steps lead to radical innovations that, taken together, lead to revolutions. Inventors take small steps without knowing what they will eventually make possible.

Deliberate attempts to take big steps can either fail or stall because other inventors have not yet taken the radical or incremental steps necessary. Leonardo da Vinci designed plans for flying machines in the thirteenth century but these were not possible without the advances in aerodynamic and manufacturing knowledge of the late nineteenth century. Armed with this knowledge, many inventors competed to make manned flight practical.

They can also fail because the people trying to take the big steps are not aware of small inventions that they need. Philosopher-inventors designed telescopes in Ancient Greece but could not build them because they did not mix with the artisans who made the glass they needed.

Some innovations are **dependent** on other innovations or conditions. The electric light bulb is of no use without an electric light system including wiring, generators, power stations, and companies to maintain them. Other innovations are more **independent**, either because they are standalone or because the conditions for their success are already present. The first piece of sharpened flint qualifies as independent. Nearly all modern innovations are dependent on something else but not always on other innovations. Knowing what your idea relies on is vital to its success.

The focus of the innovation also varies:

- **Product** innovations involve new products and new characteristics of old products. The process that makes them may be much the same but the product has changed incrementally or radically.
- **Process** innovation refers to new ways of doing something. The product may be the same but the way of producing is new, better, more efficient or more reliable. Computer-aided design and manufacture are process innovations.
- **Organisational** innovation finds new ways of structuring and managing people. The product and process may be the same but the way of organising people has changed. Bureaucracy, adhocracy, meritocracy are all ways of organising.

These areas of focus are often interrelated. New ways of organising people can make it possible to produce new products and follow new processes. New products can require new processes. New processes make new products possible.

In all these ways of looking at innovation, the definition remains the same. It is new stuff considered useful by someone. It can be incremental, radical or revolutionary. It can be dependent or independent. It can change products, services, processes or organisations. In fact, it can change anything. Any belief. Any situation. Any nation. Any planet. Which is why understanding and getting better at innovation is vital to our shared future.

TRUTH

2

A beautiful idea is never perfect

There is no such thing as the perfect business idea. There are good ideas that reward effort. The best ideas attract interest and inspire support. Beautiful ideas change our perception of what is possible and what is desirable. People invest hope, time and money in attempting to make beautiful ideas real.

You can always improve a worthwhile idea. Either the detail of the idea can be bettered or the implementation of the idea can be enhanced. Anything useful can be made more useful. Anything desirable can be made more desirable. Any practical limits may never be reached and certainly not in your lifetime. At the point that an idea approaches perfection, fashion and expectations surge ahead, leaving the innovator with considerable room to find further improvements.

Wal-Mart, K-Mart and Target all launched in the same year—1962—with the same idea. Discount retailing brought them all success but in different ways and at different times. The idea was simply to offer big brands at discount prices but has been tweaked, sculpted and shaped by circumstance *and* creativity.

Attention K-Mart shoppers—K-Mart boomed initially but failed to re-invest in technology or store concepts. At first, famous for its "blue light specials" complete with flashing police lights and in-store announcements drawing attention to time-limited bargains. Later, famous for cheap, drab, dirty stores, falling behind rivals, declaring bankruptcy, firing thousands of workers and merging with Sears Roebuck.

Always Low Prices, Always—Wal-Mart surged ahead with its slogan "Always Low Prices, Always" using its investment in state-of-the-art technology to reduce the cost of products from production to sale. It became the largest company in the world by revenue before growth slowed. Younger customers wanted a more luxurious, less corporate experience. Many non-American customers wanted quality and conscience ahead of low prices.

Expect More, Pay Less—Target has focused on offering high quality goods at low prices rather than cheap merchandise at dramatically low prices. This has attracted younger, more affluent customers who affectionately refer to the store as "Tar-zhay" with a

French pronunciation to emphasise its boutique aspirations. Top fashion and product designers work with Target to develop exclusive ranges at value prices. The company maintains an extensive network of suppliers and trend spotters who provide information about what should be on their shelves. There are no in-store announcements or piped music. Instead, you will find cafés, banks, pharmacies, wider aisles and more aesthetically pleasing store design. It gives the impression of acting on ethical issues before public opinion or legislation forces them to comply. For the moment, it is leading the way with its interpretation of the discount idea.

A powerful idea, well expressed, is difficult to stop over time. Innovators want to deliver the promised benefits of the idea. They keep trying until the idea becomes practical and popular. People want what the idea promises and are willing to support the latest, greatest attempt to put the idea into practice. This mixture of individual dedication, often without reward, and mass-market interest in the possibilities inherent in the idea combine to provide innovation with enduring impetus.

The founder of Wal-Mart used to visit his rivals with a little tape-recorder to steal ideas but Target still managed to deliver the discount concept in a better way. The founder of Staples sent undercover teams to his rivals so that he could find out about their weaknesses but missed the strengths that led to Office Depot overtaking them. The founder of Dell found ways of delivering Hewlett-Packard's most profitable products for much lower prices but forgot to deliver their quality so within a few years had fallen behind again. Ideas need constant renewal.

A great idea will never be perfect and will never work perfectly in all markets and all seasons. Wal-Mart has imported its complete blueprint to Japan, including an automated distribution centre with five miles of conveyor belts, an in-store computer system and low prices. It has also imported a certain disregard for national differences and replaced Japanese managers with American executives with no experience outside of the American Wal-Mart family. The result has been $1 billion invested and about the same amount in cumulative losses. Japanese employees fought back over the way they were treated and Japanese consumers object to their favourite tastes and brands disappearing from the shelves—even if the replacements are cheaper.

By complete contrast, 7-Eleven has grown to become the biggest chain in the world, with 1000 more outlets than McDonald's. Its idea is convenience shopping. The concept started when a dock employee from Texas started selling bread and milk to other employees. In the 1980s, Japanese investors bought the chain and helped the format expand to 18 countries. Its history has taught it that the convenience idea travels well internationally as long as it is adapted to reflect local tastes. Each country works with franchised partners who share 50 per cent of the profits and contribute local knowledge that delivers convenience appropriate to local tastes.

> ## All good ideas recognise opportunities and meet needs.

All good ideas recognise opportunities and meet needs. Some variations on a specific idea can be protected legally in some countries for a few years, but no idea can be protected for long, and big ideas can rarely be protected at all. And since the idea that you try to protect isn't perfect there is nothing to stop anyone doing something better. The only response is to keep improving on your idea, particularly in ways that are difficult for competitors to believe or understand.

Amazon thrived because it implemented the online bookstore idea better than any of its early rivals did, not because it was the only company to have the idea or the first company to have the idea. It continues to grow *only* because it keeps trying to improve on the details of the idea and the way it puts it into practice. The name changed—from cadabra.com. The concept changed—from bookshop to trusted adviser and retail community. The product reviews, the wireless e-book reader, the free video previews and its own search engine: all enhancements to the original idea that will never be perfect.

In the real world, there are no ideas that conform absolutely to the description or definition of an ideal type. There are no ideas complete beyond practical or theoretical improvement. There are no ideas that exactly fit customers" needs ever or for ever. There are no ideas entirely without flaws, defects or shortcomings. This is good news for anyone who wants to contribute and for any business that wants to grow.

TRUTH

3

A crisis is a terrible thing to waste

Samsung preaches the gospel of perpetual crisis. That's why 40 per cent of employees work in research and development looking for the next breakthrough. That's why deadlines are never changed. It's why design teams volunteer to live and work 24 hours a day in their Innovation Center. They pursue perfection against the clock until they deliver. The result? Over 1600 patents each year, the industry's lowest costs and highest profits, and weekly announcements of the "world's first" or "world's best".

People need some reason to make tough choices. Organisations find it even harder to make progress without knowing that it "has to", and will usually wait until a real crisis comes along before getting on with the hard stuff that is essential to moving forward.

A crisis is not the same as a disaster (although a disaster may prompt a crisis). It is a "crucial or decisive point or situation" or a "turning point". Such turning points force a choice between inertia and innovation. When faced with a crisis, ask: How can we use this crisis to inspire innovation?

> A crisis is not the same as a disaster (although a disaster may prompt a crisis).

IKEA's history is a sequence of such choices. Competition with other mail order firms led to its first showroom. Supplier boycotts led to it designing and building its own furniture. Transportation problems led to the flat pack concept. A showroom fire led to a much bigger showroom concept. Insufficient numbers of sales people at the showroom launch led to the self-service idea. It would have been easy to waste each crisis but instead they inspired innovation.

Waiting for a real crisis to drive innovation may not allow enough time or resources for new ideas to save the company. By the time anyone recognises a real crisis, it may be too late to do anything about it. Even if the company survives, the real crisis does not

> By the time anyone recognises a real crisis, it may be too late to do anything about it.

happen often enough to motivate continuous improvement, progress or growth.

■ **You can look into the future.** What may endanger your company? What products could your competitors launch? What new laws may challenge the way your company does business? How will customer-needs develop? What do you have to do better to thrive in the future?

■ **You can look into the past.** What has threatened your company in previous years? What has killed other similar companies? What threats have there been to your country? Or your division?

■ **You can look at the present**. What events of the day encourage a sense of urgency? How will political victories or losses impact on your plans? How do new discoveries challenge your markets? What can you learn from the successes and failures of others?

Intel also believes in using crisis to drive innovation. Since computers don't really wear out, the only way to convince customers to buy a new one is to make it twice as good. To achieve this, Intel aims to double the speed of its computer chips every two years. It decided that the only way of innovating fast enough was to use fear of future events to motivate urgent focus. It did this by encouraging what it calls a "culture of paranoia". Everyone worried about real and imagined threats. Everyone practised "constructive confrontation" to express opinions bluntly in order to subject proposals to aggressive, desk-thumping, red-faced criticism. All in the hope that it would force tough action before a real crisis wiped out the company.

There are limitations to such a culture. Being paranoid may mean that you notice threats but it does not mean that you know what to do about them. Nor does it mean that you can get the company to do what you think has to be done.

Paranoid Intel has known for decades that its success in chips for personal computers was getting in the way of developing new chips for other gadgets. It has tried and failed many times to do anything about the impending crisis. Yelling is not the same as open discussion. Vitriol is not an effective replacement for reasoned argument. Is it likely that people with the most valuable opinions will also be those with the loudest voices? Won't managers be most likely to win?

The strength of the Samsung approach to "crisis culture" is that it builds in urgency and focus at the start of the project. This is where it has the greatest impact. First, it seeks to avoid the main reasons innovations fail—because they are late or incomplete. Second, simplifying and improving the design at the start helps every stage of production. Third, it only demands paranoia from small groups over a short period. This is crisis culture that is attempting to be effective, flexible and sustainable.

TRUTH

4

A great innovation deserves a great name

In 1939, two physicists announced what they called a "gravitationally completely collapsed object". The world yawned. Forty years later, when a lecturer commented that it deserved a better name, a member of the audience suggested renaming it a "black hole". The name stuck. This time the world woke up and the name became part of our working vocabulary.

The name given to an innovation matters. A great innovation may survive without a great name but the name helps. Particularly if the innovation is also a product, a service, something you will be trying to sell, something that needs a brand.

The name given to an innovation matters.

Names are valuable. Dell bought Alienware, a high-end PC producer popular with gamers. Dell could have designed high-end computers but people don't associate Dell with high performance. No one wears Dell t-shirts. People buy Alienware clothing. It's cool.

Instead of calling its new processor the "586", Intel named it the Pentium. It turned the microprocessor from an invisible component into a visible difference between computers. It also made its competitors look old-fashioned.

Having a good name for your innovation doesn't guarantee success. Calling Sega's games console Dreamcast didn't stop it losing to Sony's Playstation. Zune is a good name for a media player but

Having a good name for your innovation doesn't guarantee success.

Microsoft still hasn't overtaken the iPod. The same was true of Segway, Motorola's Rokr, Apple's Newton and Nokia's N-Gage.

A next-generation product gives you a choice. Should you continue with an existing name? Or choose a new name? Customers have a soft spot for innovation but they are also suspicious. They are concerned about the effort in learning to use something new. They are also wary about problems found in new products.

New names promote newness. For the majority of customers, this triggers different assumptions about the risks and rewards of buying the new product. Customers may judge the newness of the product on the newness of the name, *not* on other information available. If a product has changed radically to appeal to non-customers then a new name may be the only way to get across the message.

Hard-core gamers reacted angrily to the Wii console name but Nintendo successfully targeted people who *did not use* consoles. Many criticised the name but the company gained valuable attention from non-gamers. Nintendo had two powerful stories ready to explain the new brand. First, that Wii meant gaming for groups, as in "we are all included". Second, that Wii meant "overthrow of the gods", as in Sony and Microsoft, in ancient Japanese.

Understanding probable customer reactions allows you to design marketing to manage those reactions. Products with new names, particularly bizarre new names, benefit more from extended guarantees or trial periods than price discounts. Kia, the Korean car manufacturer, called its new hatchback the *C"eed* and sells it with a seven-year warranty. The message is—our cars are surprising *in a good way*.

Existing names promote continuity. Customers expect the new product to be easy to learn, to have no problems and to be "better" than the old version. Non-customers are less likely to notice the new features and customers may be unhappy if the new product is a radical innovation hiding under an old name.

When the taste of Coke was changed, many customers were shocked. They did not want a radically different taste when they brought their traditional favourite. Coke brought back the old taste just three months later. The new *taste* was not the problem—the problem was putting the new taste in bottles with an old name.

Some of the best names for new products have come from unlikely sources. A freelancer working at Apple proposed the iPod name after the prototype reminded him of the white pods from the spaceship in *2001: A Space Odyssey*.

Naming consultancies can ensure that names are available as trademarks and websites, and that they don't mean anything rude in another country. They can market test different names but they cannot guarantee that the name will help the product.

There are other ways of sending the message that a product is innovative. In fact, the message and packaging can be the innovation that seems useful. We know the Mini and Beetle are new because they look new—a name change would be wasteful. Making a product look innovative is the single best way of getting the message across. That's why the Dyson vacuum cleaner looks like a science fiction weapon. The name becomes innovative because it is associated with the design.

There are four critical issues:

- **Character**: What is this new thing like? How does it work? What does it solve? Does it do what the name suggests? *Egg* is a bank that provides safety for your "nest egg". *Facebook* puts friends into an electronic version of a university face-book. *Blu-ray* DVD highlights the use of blue lasers to create bigger capacity discs.

- **Customers**: Who are they? Why will they buy? What attracts them? *Digg* is a website that allows bloggers to post up, and vote on, articles. The name appeals to people who want others to "dig" their expertise. *Alligator Poo* is a crystalline sweet that appeals to its teen audience *and* causes a reaction from their parents!

- **Competition**: What other names are there? How can you be different? How can you avoid a generic name? *EasyJet* and *JetBlue* both offered innovative low-cost air travel, and when they launched their names were distinctive compared to traditional airlines with their national and regional names.

- **Communication**: How can you tell the story? How can you deliver the message? Sometimes the story behind the naming process is what matters. *Starbucks* combined the name of the first mate in *Moby Dick* with the name of a mining camp near Seattle with a mermaid in its logo. It has very little directly to do with the concept of a "third place" coffee shop and yet somehow evokes just such a feeling of literature and exotic products from far-off places.

Sadly, there is no certain way of picking a winning name for an innovation. The best names often only seem smart after they are successful. *Ebay got its name when the web address its founder wanted, "Echo Bay", was unavailable. Apple got its name because its founder thought it was the perfect fruit.* Even so, putting in effort to pick a good name and expertise to avoid a bad name is worthwhile. A great name can allow an okay innovation to become a great brand.

TRUTH

5

Any fool can do either, genius does both

Ask a child to choose between ice cream and chocolate cake. The answer is usually "both". Adults are much the same. We don't want the disadvantages of our choices. We want cheaper *and* better, cars without pollution, not cars *or* pollution, more time *and* more money.

Innovation promises benefits without all of the costs. The aim is to have your cake *and* eat it. If the innovation doesn't overcome some contradiction between conflicting objectives then it isn't genius, it's obvious. The more obvious it is the less protection it offers from competition, even if it is very popular. The most successful products deliver two benefits that contradict each other.

> The most successful products deliver two benefits that contradict each other.

Linux is one of the few operating systems that can challenge Windows. It can challenge Microsoft for two reasons: it is free to buy and it is open. Charging nothing and allowing anyone to customise the product has encouraged many companies to use it instead of paying upgrade fees. Corporate customers do not have to choose between paying a lot and having an operating system that works. They can have both—or at least it looks that way.

Years ago, guests had to bring their own shampoo to a hotel if they wanted any during their stay. They also had to choose between personal service from small hotels and luxurious facilities in large hotels. This changed when a hotel owner in Canada was unwilling to accept the compromise. He reasoned that it was possible for a medium-sized hotel to provide luxurious facilities by providing such remarkable service that guests would pay a greater share of the cost of providing them. This included being the first to provide complimentary shampoo to guests. The Four Seasons hotel chain's huge global success is the result of his desire to provide both, *not* either.

The new CEO of PepsiCo, Indra Nooyi, is a health food enthusiast running the world's second largest maker of sugar-filled carbonated drinks. Since joining, she has expressed her dissatisfaction with the conflict between health and pleasure. She wants to sell food that is "fun for you" *and* "good for you". To overcome the contradiction between these two objectives she has introduced health food products *and* developed healthy versions of existing bestsellers. Pepsi's efforts are not just ethical or creative. They are necessary. Meanwhile, Nestlé, a key competitor, is transforming itself from a food company to a food *and* health *and* nutrition company. It is designing and launching foods designed to cure medical conditions. The present includes omega-three-enriched milkshakes; the future will bring anti-cancer smarties.

Innovators are willing to think widely about alternatives to the obvious. Many of them have backgrounds that make it easier. The man who started the Linux project is the son of radical journalists, grandson of a poet, and a member of the Swedish-speaking minority in Finland. The leader of Pepsi is an Indian woman leading an American company who played guitar in a rock band and cricket in an era and culture when many viewed physical exertion as unseemly for a girl.

Each innovation attempts to reconcile the irreconcilable. The mindset behind these innovations does not accept that the first answer is the best answer, because the first answer is usually obvious. The first answer is what you get when you ask "why" things are the way they are. The better answer comes when you keep asking "why?" and then ask "why not?"

> Each innovation attempts to reconcile the irreconcilable.

Asking these questions is what has allowed Honda to launch a car powered by hydrogen fuel cells that produces *no pollution*. It was not willing to accept the compromise between two opposing characteristics. Asking these questions is what will allow you to see a combination of attractive features and see how to overcome unattractive compromises. Cirque du Soleil is just circus without cold tents and stale popcorn. Net Jet is just a private plane without the cost of ownership. Be wary of innovation that can't shake off obvious compromises: Concorde was super quick but only for the super rich. New space planes may be able to travel from London to Sydney in two hours but if it costs the estimated $130,000 the compromise will keep the market small and the service unprofitable.

If you ask these questions, some people will complain. They fear that the answers will cause more work and make their heads hurt. Yet without questions that reveal the connections between things it is difficult to improve anything. Asking "why?" and "why not?" will question the assumptions of specialists and experts. This is uncomfortable for people who have enjoyed the comfort of standard answers and the protection of their profession. They may dismiss your ability to understand well enough to have an opinion. It is liberating to those who want to grasp what is really happening and improve it. They may welcome your ability to have an opinion that increases their understanding.

TRUTH

6

All new ideas are made of old ideas

About 430 BC, the Greek philosopher Democritus wondered how many times you could break a piece of matter in half and in half again. He concluded that everything in existence is made of what he named atoms—or átomos. It was a bloody great insight: everything and everyone is made of atoms.

Each new life consists of old atoms. You don't get new atoms—not even when you were a baby. You get old atoms that have been around for 15 billion years. What's surprising is that even though you are almost completely made of just three types of atom you are unique. Your seven billion, billion, billion hydrogen, oxygen and carbon atoms are identical to mine. We are the same—only different.

Each new idea consists of old ideas. Originality doesn't rely on creating something from nothing. It relies on putting together ideas and materials in new ways. At its best, this process meets existing needs with new ideas or even creates new needs from old ideas.

Pizza Hut pizzas are the same as Domino's pizzas—only different. Burger King's hamburgers are the same as McDonald's hamburgers. A BMW is the same as a Ford. Wal-Mart stores are the same as Nordstrom stores. Nike shoes are the same as Gucci shoes. Only different.

Originality doesn't rely on creating something from nothing. It relies on putting together ideas and materials in new ways.

Atoms behave in very different ways depending on how they connect to each other. There are infinite possible combinations—including the blueprint for life, sugar, phosphate and hydrogen, glued together to form the famous double helix molecule of DNA.

Life, evolution and innovation can only rearrange what already exists.

Life, evolution and innovation can only rearrange what already exists. Mice and elephants, sharks and penguins, the blue whale and the flea, the chimpanzee and man, all share the same atomic composition—the same stuff. Their dramatic diversity in weight, size, colour, texture and behaviour comes about because the basic building blocks combine in different ways.

Nintendo made its new idea for the Wii games console from lots of old ideas. Cartoon characters of players came from the old idea of Kokeshi, traditional Japanese wooden dolls. The Wii remote is packed full of old off-the-shelf ideas, including the amazing accelerometer chip. It lets you swing a baseball bat, tennis racket or light sabre. There's even the old idea of families playing together! The result is the new idea of the virtual family playroom.

The story of civilisation is the story of making new ideas from old ideas. Your ancestors noticed forest fire and learned to control it. Fire combined with tree trunks to create wooden boats. Someone took the idea of round discs from pottery to make wooden wheels and stuck them on wooden boats to create the horse-drawn cart. In 1672, a Jesuit priest in China added the old idea of carts to the old idea of steam to create a miniature automobile as a toy for the emperor's son. And at 4:17:42 p.m. Eastern Daylight Time, on 20 July 1969, the old ideas of ships, fireworks and science fiction were added together to allow the first moon landing.

New art, literature and music are constantly recycled from old ideas. The genius is in mixing them together into something even better. Shakespeare took traditional dramatic structures, themes, poems, prose and street language, and used them to create better drama and 1700 new words. Music producers take ideas, riffs, beats and vocals from old music and create something fresh—Mashup or bastard pop. The R&B vocal from Destiny's Child singing "Bootylicious" is mixed with Nirvana's grunge metal 'smells Like Teen Spirit" to produce the Mashup classic 'smells Like Booty". Cirque du Soleil is just the circus in a theatre—two old ideas combined to create a worldwide phenomenon.

Knowing that innovators make new ideas from old ideas means you won't try to start from nothing. You can't anyway. All your ideas come from something you already know. Not trying to start from nothing saves time. Working with existing knowledge helps you to build something better. Recombining what already exist increases the novelty of your ideas. You know it's something new. It increases the practicality of your ideas. You know its components already work.

And it boosts the chances that people will accept it
because it's the same—only different.

TRUTH

7

Bet small to win big

You've seen the big picture, haven't you? The typical big company wants big products. They want big ideas. If they're big shots with big balls then they place big bets on a big future. No one wants the small project. Or to be the small project manager. Who wants to do that?

The problem with the big bet approach is that you are limited to a small number of guesses. You are forced to choose too early. Judging winners and losers before the race begins. Putting all your eggs in one big basket. Or worse—putting all your faith in one egg.

> Most of us accept the common-sense notion that risk should be spread.

Most of us accept the common-sense notion that risk should be spread. For some reason it is hard for most companies to spread that risk by sharing out the "risk dollars" between many small projects. Some leaders seem to find it easier to bet big on their own hunches than to bet on their people.

A few years ago, Whirlpool decided to make a big bet on innovation by making hundreds of little bets. Instead of investing half a million dollars each on a few ideas it learned how to take smaller calculated risks. The choice was no longer all or nothing. It was $20 million in 400 bite-size chunks of $25,000. Enough money to test ideas, engage small teams of people and do enough learning to inform future funding decisions. The little bets now bring in $1 billion a year.

Betting big has other, less obvious, disadvantages:

- Most of the time, a big project develops a life of its own. No one wants to take the decision to write-off all the money wasted so far so it becomes a zombie project—using up resources years after it is unnecessary or unwanted.

- Often by the time a big project is completed the advantages of starting it are no longer relevant. Competitor products have overtaken the original objectives so that even if the big project succeeds it will fail.

- Bizarrely, a big project is less likely to have rigorous criteria for investment than a small project. A big boss does not have to justify his big decisions. And, a big decision is less clearly defined than a small decision because there is simply more of it to define.

Betting small helps in a number of ways:

- The safest investments are those that start to pay off soonest. Even better are those that inform the next round of investment decisions. A small project may develop into a big project having contributed to the success of the company.

- The small bet allows more people to contribute. It engages their talents and goodwill. It encourages them to experiment with comfortable levels of responsibility.

- Not all ideas require huge amounts of funding to take to market, or benefit from a large amount of money in the early stages of development. They can be ruined by the weight of expectation and the rush to justify expenditure.

Toyota believes in betting small to win big. In one year, its employees suggested over 750,000 ideas for improvement. The company then implemented over 80 per cent! In isolation, most suggestions were small and incremental. The total impact of three quarters of a million improvements is to strengthen Toyota's culture of innovation—getting better is a habit gained through repetition.

Sony's success with the Walkman showed another side of betting small to win big. It did not know which combination of features would most appeal to customers so it developed over two hundred different models each available in different colours. The resulting thousands of variants each represented a small bet that allowed them to find out what customers wanted by offering them choice.

All or nothing bets are only wise when the future is certain. If winning is certain then bet everything. If there's nothing to lose then bet everything. Since the future is not certain the best choice today is usually the one that will leave you free to make most choices tomorrow. This is because

> All or nothing bets are only wise when the future is certain.

you do not know what choices will be attractive tomorrow. You may change. You may learn something new. The future will change what works and what does not.

Too many attempts to innovate fail because all the resources are used up before the successful solution, the magic formula, is found. Making as many small bets as possible increases the number of attempts possible and keeps options open.

TRUTH

8

Better to ask forgiveness than permission

Breaking the rules is part of the creative process: not *all* of the time and not *all* of the rules, but being creative means doing something different. Some of the rules are unspoken. Some appear to be common sense. Some are formal and come with sanctions attached. Doing something different is often only possible if you bend, break and ignore rules.

Most innovation involves breaking or bending rules. Not rule breaking that is unethical or dishonest, but rule breaking that is necessary to getting ideas designed, built and out of the door. Rules are helpful—they allow us to work together. Standardisation is useful—it allows products to work together. However, rules can also get in the way of experimentation, improvement and breakthrough innovation.

> Rules can get in the way of experimentation, improvement and breakthrough innovation.

Enforcing rules appeals to managers who think it's their job to get other people to conform, obey and follow without question. It's simple. You lay down the law, keep an eye on your potential criminals and then punish them if they step out of line. The problem is that people stop trying to get the job done. Smart people become depressed if they have to do what makes no sense to them. Even if they try, the rules slow performance and often make innovation impossible.

Turning a blind eye to rule breaking allows the team to avoid the restraints of the rule and the project to get the benefit that brings. It also allows the manager to avoid having to challenge a rule. The problem is that it means rules don't change to help future projects. It also means that people who break the rules to try to get the project delivered risk sanctions—especially if the project fails.

Challenging rules can be costly. It takes time to argue for the change. Time you either don't want to spend or can't spare. It risks bringing sanctions against the rule breaker. Gaining extra attention means you follow the rules because people are paying attention. You may find yourself labelled as a troublemaker. Not challenging rules means that the company doesn't learn. Efforts to improve have to survive illogical and unhelpful restraints chaining them to the past.

The only companies that don't have to break rules to innovate are those who make it easy to challenge rules! They make it simple and worthwhile to raise concerns. They encourage rule modifying as part of improvement. You don't have to ask to change something; they ask what you want to change. Such openness about challenging rules is relatively rare. It requires the company to accept the limits of rules, a system for rule modification, and high levels of trust that the system will be fast, intelligent, bold and supportive.

How do you know when to break the rules? Some people can't help themselves—they are natural-born rule-breakers. Some aren't aware of how often they ignore etiquette, defy best practice and break conventions. Some are aware but follow their own rules anyway. Others feel driven to break the rules by their commitment to finding a better way.

If you know why certain rules need to be broken it might help people understand why you have broken them. If you weigh the risks of breaking the rules, you can decide whether you are willing to pay the price. Knowing the reason for a rule is worthwhile. You might think something is getting in the way but find out that it was protecting something important. Find out if there is a way of breaking rules that is acceptable or even praiseworthy. 3M only promotes people who have stuck their necks out. Bill Gates likes people with the guts to shout back at him.

Find out if there is a way of breaking rules that is acceptable or even praiseworthy.

Skunkworks groups have leaders and team members who are all natural rule-breakers. They are separate from the main rule-following organisation so bureaucracy or politics does not slow them down. The original Skunkworks designed a revolutionary new jet in one month and had it in production after only 143 days.

Bootlegging involves motivated people secretly organising the innovation process. It's for the benefit of the company but done without permission. It isn't part of the plan and it receives no official resources. Honda engineers designed and built a replacement for its MR2 sports car unofficially because they were unimpressed with the official design.

Some rules have outlived their usefulness. Some rules were never very useful. Some rules have exceptions. Some are just not appropriate for particular situations. Smart people know the difference. Very smart companies let people judge whether to modify a rule *so that breaking* a company rule is no longer necessary.

TRUTH

9

Creativity is a process not an accident

Some people make coming up with new ideas look easy. They just open their mouths and, as if by magic, originality appears. For others, the opposite is true. They think of creativity as something that other people do. They have never had an idea and couldn't be creative if their lives or jobs depended on it.

It's tempting to believe that people are just born creative or non-creative. It's a commonly held view that having creativity is mysterious and unknowable. Perhaps this is because many make the mistake of concentrating on the "eureka" moment itself and ignoring the creative process that leads up to it.

New ideas do not appear from nowhere. It's just that the work needed to produce them tends to be behind the scenes and in the heads of creative people. They follow certain steps and share particular behaviours—anyone can learn enough about them to improve their own creative ability.

New ideas do not appear from nowhere.

Creative people love ideas. They collect them. They enjoy ideas from different places and about very diverse subjects. They are curious and passionate about many, many topics. They chat knowledgeably about a range of interests, from sports, world politics, quantum physics and the latest Hollywood gossip to gardening tips, ballet and martial arts. Their curiosity is immense.

Creative people also love to play around with the ideas that they collect. For them everything is connected—part of an overall pattern. Old ideas are moved around, combined, squeezed and stretched to make new ideas.

It may seem obvious to say so, but the good news is that the creative process has simple steps. Don't let their obviousness or simplicity stop you from thinking about how treating idea creation as a process can help.

The first step is collecting together old ideas—or existing facts. You need to know as much as possible about the world in general *and* get a solid, deep working knowledge of the facts that surround the need for a new idea. This may seem daunting or unnecessary but facts are the raw material for innovation.

Everything is connected and there are relationships between all facts. Just accepting this principle will make anyone more creative. Facts stop being walls to stop progress and turn into building blocks to allow progress. They can be

Everything is connected and there are relationships between all facts.

rearranged into endless new combinations. The only practical limit is your knowledge of the facts and your ability to see relationships between them.

Seeking insights from old facts is hard work. It requires playfulness but it's still demanding. The intellectual effort, and time, involved means that some people stop too early. The trick is to continue until there are enough alternatives, enough partial ideas noted down and in memory. Eventually, after consciously wrestling with so many different ways of rearranging ideas around a particular need, or circumstance, things will get confused. No one idea stands out from the rest. Nothing is clear.

Now is the time to allow your subconscious to make one great idea from all the raw material and unfinished ideas. The best way of doing this is to do something completely different. Put the books away, stop talking about your idea, have a nap, go and enjoy yourself, reintroduce yourself to your friends. There is little to gain by returning to the problem until your mind has cleared.

The idea will arrive only after the mind receives space and time. It will seem to have come from nowhere—as a flash of inspiration—but you will know that it is the result of following a deliberate process. This means that idea creation can become repeatable. Knowing that it is repeatable means you can improve.

The final step is to make your great idea practical and profitable. Many ideas stop looking so attractive. They start looking like a lot of hard work with no certain reward. You won't have all the skills necessary to make your idea happen. You won't even have all the knowledge needed to create a mass market out of an insight.

Your choice will be to try anyway, give up, or share your idea. Since your idea isn't finished, it will be hard to be confident enough to share. If you don't share, you risk spending time on something that doesn't work. You need to subject your idea to criticism and possibly ridicule, so take that final step out of your head and find out if it has what it takes to become an innovation.

TRUTH
10

Creativity is its own reward

Motivation comes from inside and outside. You can give people work they love or reward them for doing jobs they hate. Some people care more about the rewards and less about the job. At the other extreme, some are willing to work for no pay if it means doing something they love.

Motivation from inside is vital to creativity. If the work is unsatisfying but the rewards are motivational, then effort, *not* creative problem solving, is the best you can hope to receive. People who are motivated only by rewards will do what is necessary to get them and nothing more. Even if you reward creativity, a person not engaged with their work will be less likely to have the insights necessary to innovate.

Creativity allows people to fulfil needs that go beyond accumulating pay and promotion. People gain a sense of control over their environment and their lives. They learn more about themselves as they explore their ability to think new thoughts and put them into action. They gain satisfaction, pleasure, enjoyment through creative activity. Creativity is a source of happiness—even if that sounds idealistic nonsense, it's still true. Deep involvement with a task, the opportunity to do your best work and the freedom to make a difference are intrinsically rewarding.

> Creativity is a source of happiness—even if that sounds idealistic nonsense, it's still true.

It follows that being given only superficial influence, being prevented from improving something, being stopped from doing work you are proud of is fundamentally depressing. If people are interrupted continually, they will never get the flow they need to gain pleasure from their work. If people believe someone will prevent them doing their best work then they will stop trying. What is the point? Why be disappointed? Why make an effort only to see that effort wasted? If your business or team is missing deadlines, falling behind the competition or churning out sub-standard products, you should look at what is blocking creativity instead of assuming that your people are the problem.

Looking outside for rewards is more likely to lead to conformity. People want to fit in more than they want to do creative work. People who desperately want to do creative work are less likely to accept the constraints of conformity. They are paying more attention to the demands of the task than to how they look to the people around them. The greater the opportunities for creativity the less emphasis the group will place on conforming. The more the individuals in a group are convinced that the situation encourages creativity the less likely they are to play political or ego-driven games.

Of particular interest are individuals who are motivated, more or less equally, by intrinsic rewards from the work *and* extrinsic rewards from some external source. It's a large group and they make their choices dependent on their beliefs about the likelihood of attaining either kind of reward. The more you can encourage people to think about the intrinsic rewards of making a difference the more creative they are. The possibility of attaining the creativity *high* or *flow* is highly motivational and effective at unlocking the memory or the ability to create.

Thinking about extrinsic rewards blocks creativity. Dwelling on what people will say about you or what you will get for your efforts reduces the creative urge. Writers, advertisers, inventors and anyone else who focuses on the critics and the awards ceremonies find it hard to put pen to paper. You will look for safety, for tradition, for what you think you should be doing. Your attention divides between the demands of the task and the rewards following its completion. You will not find creativity because for every step you take towards it, you take another step back.

External rewards can still help. *If* the rewards system builds trust in the process then people can relax and focus on creative problem solving. *If* you reward creativity and it is clear what kind of solution is wanted then people will feel motivated and able to take clear steps towards the goal. The problem is that to make it simple you have to do a lot of the creative work before you ask the question or figure out the reward. This is only

Creativity increases when you let people do the work they love.

possible for some aspects of some tasks and doesn't include solutions that you haven't even considered. If you want extrinsic rewards to work effectively then you have to do your homework first.

People are more likely to love their work when they are able to do it creatively, without interference, and to a high standard. Creativity increases when you let people do the work they love.

TRUTH

11

Crowds are mad, bad and advantageous to know

You've figured out that collaboration is a good thing. You recognise some of the possibilities for mass collaboration. Getting more brains engaged in solving more problems is your objective. All those people. All those ideas. If you could get them working together, you could harness the wisdom of crowds.

You want to get the right people interested, working on the right problem until they find workable solutions. You don't want involving mass participants to be more pain or more costly than it's worth. You don't want looking outside for answers to delay internal efforts to find what works. You want to minimise the effort of managing the group and ensure that the solution from the crowd is *better* than the solution you could have found without their help.

■ **The prize** offered for solving a well-defined but very difficult problem is not new but it is powerful. In 1783, the king of France offered a prize for a method of producing alkali from sea salt. In 1714, the UK government offered a prize for a simple, reliable method of determining exact longitude. The French Society for the Encouragement of Industry offered a prize for the development of the first commercial hydraulic turbine. In 2004, the Ansari X-Prize paid $10 million to the winner of its challenge to make the first private flight into space. In 2006, Google became sponsors of a $30 million prize for a robotic space mission. Prizes generate healthy publicity that pulls potential innovators towards the problem. Teams learn from each other's public attempts to achieve the objectives of the prize. Teams can attract additional investors to fund the research so that the overall research budget exceeds the prize fund.

■ **The living document** allows people to change, comment on, contribute to and criticise a proposed solution. The initial question and answer do not need to be correct—they just need to be of interest to the group with the expertise. In our electronic era, the living document may take many forms, from a shared text file to a blog or a wiki. The distinctive thing is that editing is open so readers become collaborators. Editing is transparent so that the document's evolution has a history that offers learning and knowledge about what logic leads to a particular version or decision. You capture and enhance the memory of the crowd with its wisdom in shaping different elements of a solution.

- **The community** forms around the initial problem or opportunity. It may self-organise according to the interests of the participants who take responsibility for structure and process. Linux, the free-to-use Windows competitor, and Firefox, the free-to-use internet browser, are both self-organised communities that produce material valuable to the participants. There are also many examples of paid organisers attempting to direct the activities of the group. They seek to exploit the network's insights directly from ideas or to extract valuable concepts from suggestions. **Crowdcasting** is a variant of a community in which the organisers are paid by companies who want ideas and thinking from large groups of informed people. Hilton Hotels and American Express have run innovation competitions with MBA students organised by Idea Crossing. **Crowdsourcing** is a second variant that offers tasks and problems to the public. Innocentive enables 100,000 scientists to respond to challenges issued by various organisations. Amazon offers paid tasks to people that appear to customers to be the results of computerised artificial intelligence. **Co-creation** is a third variant that involves customers in designing, testing and decision making. Communities reward their participants in various ways: financially, in respect, or in satisfaction. They can be individuals, professionals, amateurs or companies.

- **The market** is an attempt to benefit from the overall wisdom, or composite judgement, of the crowd. Most people will be wrong about predicting events but individual errors tend to even out across a large group. This only really works for predictions when individuals are reasonably independent because they don't know each other or because they can maintain their intellectual distance. Prediction markets work by asking individuals what they think groups will do: Who do you think will win the next election? Which product do you think other people will buy?

> You capture and enhance the memory of the crowd with its wisdom in shaping different elements of a solution.

Involving crowds in your innovation efforts is valuable but not without difficulty. Solutions may appear attractive but involve considerable costs to bring to market. If participants receive no financial reward as part of a commercial undertaking then it is likely that they will be unable or unwilling to spend considerable time completing the work. There can also be problems protecting ideas that people have publicly, and often freely, contributed.

Individuals who are part of crowds are no more likely to be right about anything than the people who work for your company. There are experts among the crowds. There are enthusiasts who can offer insights. Some will be groupies who know too much and are too dedicated to represent the needs of the mass market. Fan groups can also be too homogeneous to offer alternative opinions. They are even more susceptible to groupthink because they have opted to associate themselves with a brand or subject. Some of them have crazy, unhelpful opinions while others have bad intentions towards you and your company.

Opening yourself up to the criticism and creativity of crowds is no riskier than staying closed and pretending to have control over your reputation. It involves different kinds of risks and benefits from an understanding of those risks. It's useful for innovation to know some of what people are saying about your product. You can learn from different opinions. Sometimes you can answer questions directly with explanations, apology, information or solutions. You can also ask their questions internally and use real customer needs to drive improvement. You can look for what people hate about your product and fix it; if they are willing to write about it maybe they are willing to pay for it. Reading and watching what people hate or love on YouTube, blogs and Facebook can inspire new products and new features. Be careful not to treat the crowd like fools or passive guinea pigs. You don't employ them so they can say what they like. They can choose to compete with you, disrespect you and mess with you.

Harnessing the power of crowds is attractive. They know stuff you

> Remembering the madness of crowds will help you benefit from their wisdom.

don't. They will be buying your product. They can help generate valuable innovation and they can help spread the word about your innovations. They can also kill your new ideas with serious criticism, aggressive campaigns, or comedy at your expense. Remembering the madness of crowds will help you benefit from their wisdom.

TRUTH

12

Cut innovation some slack

Without slack built into the organisation, efforts to innovate may fail simply because there is no spare time for thinking or resources for experimenting. Many of the world's greatest ideas arrived in spare moments, unplanned and unscheduled. People use slack to provide the chaos needed for creation.

A large company is large because it successfully innovated at some point in its history. It survives past that point for one of two reasons: either it has not yet used up the resources acquired through innovation, or it is still using its slack resources to provide the raw materials for experimentation and innovation.

A small company is small because it has not yet found and exploited a mass-market innovation. Its challenge is to use its limited resources to find the innovation needle in a haystack and stay in business while it looks. The business must choose how to use available slack. Should you bet on innovation? Should you use it in operations? Should you return it to shareholders?

Google uses slack by dividing every employee's time into 70 per cent core tasks, 20 per cent related to core pursuits but determined by the individual, and 10 per cent on far-out ideas. The San Francisco initiative for city-wide free WIFI came from far-out time, as did Google Talk, a free system for instant and voice messaging, the sponsorship of the X-Prize for the first private lunar landing, or any number of Google ideas to be found on their Google labs page.

Genentech also provide their people with 20 per cent slack innovation time. Friday nights are for company beer drinking. People celebrate achievements with parties, commemorative t-shirts and celebrity bands. The company invests half of all revenue back into research. All of this is slack. Slack provides the raw material for collaborative breakthroughs. People have time to think. They have time to solve problems with colleagues. That's why the company has successfully launched four of their 13 drugs in less than three years, and has 30 more in the pipeline that have all succeeded in their clinical trials. People have space to consider alternatives and do science right.

Slack provides the raw material for collaborative breakthroughs.

Slack is also about trusting smart people. The world is too complex to control, so the only result of attempting control is to slow down innovation. You"ll just get in the way of people's attempts to improve. Providing unscheduled time around formal responsibilities is the best way to show that you trust people to contribute. It's a lot more powerful than simply complaining about a lack of initiative.

You need to leave space in the product plan and the roadmap for stuff that no one thought of when you wrote them. Over-scheduling squeezes out spontaneity. It stops people reacting creatively to situations, problems or customers. When opportunities or possibilities come along, people are just too busy to investigate. Evidence shows that this kind of breakthrough creativity does not increase when starved of time. Moments of reflection help. Yet most people do not have the time to reflect on what they have done and how they can improve.

> Most people do not have the time to reflect on what they have done and how they can improve.

A software consultant at the CERN Institute in Switzerland used slack time and computing resources to invent the World Wide Web. An engineer at Texas Instruments used slack time and laboratory space to invent the integrated circuit that led directly to the computing revolution. An accountant working for the Fleer Chewing Gum Company in Philadelphia used slack time and raw materials to invent Bubble Gum. Not one of these inventions came from scheduled time.

Just having slack resources is not enough. If people are sitting around bored, they are less likely to innovate. If slack allows people to avoid tough decisions then it will only lead to complacency. Slack is not there to provide a barrier between the company and reality. It's there to allow experimentation. To encourage thinking that creates new products, solutions and industries.

Google time gives people 14 days a month on core tasks, four days on core pursuits with tasks determined by the individual, and two days a month on far-out ideas. How many days a month do you think far-out ideas deserve? How many days a month could you give your people? How many hours is innovation worth?

TRUTH

13

Cure apathy by sharing purpose

Overcoming apathy is the essence of leadership: getting the buggers to care. Isn't it? Sometimes this is confused with "getting the buggers to behave", but if you can only manage to get the adults to sit quietly with their legs crossed until home time you really haven't achieved much, have you?

Could your people do the same job without you? Would they work harder or slower in your absence? Do you organise them better than they would organise themselves? Do they lack key technical abilities or knowledge that you alone possess? How did they cope before you got the job? Does your existence at work overcome apathy or add to it?

The eternal problem of the human being is how to structure his waking hours, in the words of Eric Berne, in his super-cool book *The Games People Play*. It follows that the "eternal problem of the manager" is how to help employees who want to do the work as a way of avoiding boredom.

> The eternal problem of the human being is how to structure his waking hours.

They may not know it, but as a manager, you are only useful to them if you influence their continued receipt of money and provide them with a way of being emotionally fed. This means that they need to gain "as many satisfactions as possible from transactions with other members", including "rituals, pastimes, games, intimacy, and activity, designed to bring 'somatic and psychic equilibrium" through relief of tension, avoidance of noxious situations, and procurement of recognition".

If you control the salary payments they will probably "behave", but they are hardly going to dedicate themselves to the cause or come skipping into work. You will get the body only to the extent that you can monitor and control it—not the disposable, floating, discretionary talent that is only applied when the state of indifference is overcome.

Apathy is object and situation specific. A perfectly energetic, happy person in one situation can be apathetic, lethargic and even depressed in another. They can even change depending on who is in the room and what is going on in the room. There is a change in energy levels when a phone call is received. Sometimes, let's assume a loved one is calling, you see smiles and animation. Other times, perhaps it's the boss or the dentist, you will see furrowed brows and deflation.

What causes it? Stress can cause apathy. The competent leader can help by giving back control of the situation to the person who has learned to be helpless. If experience has demonstrated that effort is futile then they will stay passive when faced with the unpleasant situation or apathy-inducing manager. If you are going to lose anyway then making less effort at least means that you lose with more grace.

It's also a well-established psychological principle that inescapable punishment or unpleasant consequences lead to indifference: prison, war, disability, famine, drought and excruciating appraisals with the boss or meetings in which no suggestion is ever good enough and no answer ever correct. Those who become apathetic do so because they see the situation as a problem they have personally caused, or something that happens everywhere and always. So why try to find an alternative?

Not everyone succumbs to this so-called learned helplessness. About a third of people figure out that they can change the situation (either from inside or by leaving) and that it isn't their fault, but two-thirds are likely to become indifferent when faced with evidence that effort is futile.

A leader's task is to provide evidence that effort is worthwhile and that things can be better—both generally and particularly. In so doing, they will succeed in overcoming apathy, beating boredom and restoring purpose to people's lives.

> A leader's task is to provide evidence that effort is worthwhile and that things can be better.

14

Do what your competition won't

There's a problem with competing. You just end up fighting over the same space. The same territory. Like dogs fighting over a bone. Why not find your own space? Somewhere that doesn't interest the competition. Somewhere you can do good work for people who want to buy it.

It's easy to focus on the obvious competitors, those who are like us, those that cause us obvious pain, instead of thinking like a customer, imagining what an innovation could do for them, what they might enjoy, what they would be willing to pay for, how your service or product could amaze them.

Doing what they don't want to do is a way of creating space for your idea to grow. The paradox is that it is the limitations of an innovation that protect the innovator from the competitors. They make it unattractive to existing big players and give you time to generate cash, customers and resources. Figure out what competitors don't want to do, because it bores them, reduces their profits, goes against the grain or just looks silly.

When the One Laptop Per Child (OLPC) initiative announced its project to design, build and provide laptops for $100 to communities in developing economies it was met with apathy and aggression from many established industry players—they just didn't see any profit. But it also inspired AsusTek, a Taiwanese motherboard company, to build its own high quality, lightweight notebook with prices starting at $199—less than an iPod. Over 300,000 customers bought one within the first two months after launch. The ultra portable computer had been treated as a luxury speciality product made for rich gadget fans—the Asus created an ultra portable for the masses by doing what its competitors did not want to do.

Doing what they don't understand confuses competitors. It's one reason that younger entrepreneurs may accidentally find winning strategies—what they are doing is not necessarily difficult but doing it hurts the heads of the older

As long as customers understand the benefits, it's best that competitors don't.

executives at established companies. Mavericks have a similar advantage—they are naturally confusing to those who have made their careers by fitting in. As long as customers understand the benefits, it's best that competitors don't.

Big companies find it hard to understand casual gaming. Kids playing online fantasy games. Desperate housewives playing online domestic time-wasters like Dinner Dash. Schoolgirls chatting to their friends in online worlds like Club Penguin. They don't need specialised equipment. They are often very simple to learn. Most are played within a web browser. Many are free to use, supported by advertising. Some also sell additional functionality, game levels or features. Sites like miniclips.com offer thousands of causal games. There are more people playing them than all the console games put together and they play them for between 7 and 15 hours per week. Customers spend billions of dollars each year on them but until recently they have gone unnoticed because gaming studios didn't view them as real games. They didn't understand.

Hitting them where they ain't means offering goods and services where your competitor has no interest or presence. Maybe they are too busy with the traditional big markets or the obvious sexy middle class in emerging markets. It also refers to unsupported geography and to under-served groups or needs.

In rural India, people are starting up banks to support very specific communities. One bank offers asset-based loans to rickshaw pullers on a daily repayment plan of one year, allowing them to buy instead of forever renting. Another bank was started by a sex worker to give others like her more control over their assets. Previously they were forced to pay interest rates as high as 1500 per cent to local money lenders, now they can borrow and save money to support each other and provide better lives for themselves and their families. How long will it take global competitors to notice the need?

> Delivering something different can allow you to innovate in peace.

You can innovate to do the same thing better and compete in the same way. Alternatively, you can innovate to do something different and compete in a different way. Delivering something different can allow you to innovate in peace.

TRUTH

15

Don't get lost in translation

Two people fail with innovation projects. One motivates employees with an eccentric, colourful style but receives no funding to expand his efforts. The other easily convinces the chief executive to invest heavily in innovation—yet gains no support from employees who ignore her ego-driven calls for ideas.

Speaking one language is not enough. The first is *only* fluent in the language of the frontline, the second is gifted *only* in executive-speak. They are stuck because they can communicate with only one of the many groups they need to move from ideas to innovation. Your challenge is to find a way of communicating with all the relevant groups.

Most executives receive no rewards for innovation. It's not in their job descriptions. They don't keep their jobs for generating ideas; they keep their jobs for making more money. They are interested in making more money and doing their jobs well. Your job is to translate ideas into moneymaking schemes that your executives understand:

> Your job is to translate ideas into moneymaking schemes that your executives understand.

- How does the idea help achieve company objectives?
- How does the idea help achieve appraisal objectives?
- How does the idea help achieve personal objectives?
- How does the idea make people look good?
- How does the idea make money for the company?
- How does this help the company compete?
- What do you need to test or prove the idea?
- Why is it urgent? What happens if we don't bother?

Prepare a short document with the answers. Be tough on your own idea. Put yourself in the place of the executive. Imagine that a salesperson knocks on your door or calls you without permission. Think about how you feel about spam and junk mail. Remember painful conversations with someone obsessed with something you don't care about or understand. Try not to be that person!

Pitching ideas is a cross between an interview and getting someone to marry you. It's part business, part relationship. Do your homework. Find out what they are looking for. Chat about what they are trying to accomplish. Translate your passion and geek-like knowledge into something that a normal person would understand.

People love growth graphs and simple pictures that explain the impact of an idea.

People love growth graphs and simple pictures that explain the impact of an idea. They don't want to read what you have read, or listen to what you have heard, or go through your painful journey. They just want a story that makes sense and gets them excited. A story they can repeat to their boss. A story with clarity.

Don't go alone. It makes sense to buddy-up—to get someone on your side before you even pitch. Someone who has whatever it is that you lack. IBM's shift to the internet benefited from a self-powered project from two people. One was a net nerd; the other was a marketing executive. Together they were able to translate business and technical ideas from various audiences within IBM. The X-Box project had a self-selected team of four who had the right mix of credibility *and* knowledge about the industry, technology, power politics and timing.

The IBM team of two chose not to pitch one big idea, but instead to start building bridges between different communities so that the internet became part of the working language of the company. The language changed the climate of the conversation so that executives understood the possibilities backing them into a corner, and believed in the people who had to make it happen. The Microsoft team prepared a document and pitched it in a series of meetings. It took a rollercoaster year of highs and lows to get final approval and more than another year to launch. Both projects had to be translated over and over again. Sold and resold.

You are in love with your idea. You think it's the most obvious choice in the world. Who wouldn't do it? Why can't these jerks understand? Could your boss be more stupid if he tried? It's frustrating. Being obsessed is a good thing when it helps you to keep going against the odds. It's a bad thing when it stops you seeing that the idea means different things to different people. Someone has to build it, sell it and support it. You need their help, so speaking their language helps.

For the executive reading this, you have exactly the same problem in reverse. You need the innovation because it is usually the best way of making more money. Great ideas are good for the soul, the bank balance and the share price. The trouble you may have is in translating your goals into language that engages the people who love ideas and won't be receiving your stock options or bonuses.

Of course, the smartest executives can also translate other people's ideas into actions to deliver the growth their jobs depend on. They get knowledgeable about the technicalities *and* ask questions to discover how the proposed innovation helps. They set time aside for looking at the detail. They hang out in the labs and the retail outlets looking for hidden ideas that could make a real difference. They also make their objectives clear so that people know how to contribute.

Nissan's CEO took over at the company after it had lost money in seven of the past eight years. He needed innovation because the old ways weren't working. He chose to spend his first days and months travelling the company asking questions. When he found people blocked by bureaucracy, he gave them authority. He organised cross-functional teams with a very specific goal: propose recommendations within three months to restore profitability and future growth. He told them there were no sacred cows, no taboos and no constraints. It was slow at first, but within three months the groups had assessed 2000 ideas and completed a revival plan that succeeded within two years.

It is clear that most employees find management jargon a turn-off and that many managers find technical jargon unhelpful. However, impatience with the technical language of another group has drawbacks. If you can speak the language of another group, you gain credibility and engagement. The best ideas won't get lost in translation.

TRUTH

16

Different structural strokes for different folks

There are many different ways of organising people. Each structure has its own implications for innovation. Some slow innovation down. Some are good at supporting certain kinds of innovation but not others. It is possible to mix some of these approaches while others do not really fit comfortably together. If you know the fundamental structural choices and their innovation consequences then you will be better able to create the innovation you need.

Company structure influences innovation performance. You can put the same people in different structures and achieve very different results. Structure is not the only thing that affects innovation but it does have significant influence. Part of this is the impact of circumstance on behaviour, part of it is that certain structures come with underlying assumptions about behaviour.

Mechanistic organisations are just as you imagine them. They are rigid. Everyone has specialised roles and receives tasks, training and incentives relevant to that role. People complete tasks in isolation from overall objectives. There are rules for everything and people don't tell the truth to the boss. People pretend that the rules work and no one really does anything new.

Organic organisations are the opposite. They are fluid. People work together towards the overall goal. Tasks and roles are continually readjusted and negotiated. Everyone contributes expertise and opinions. Decisions are made by whichever groups are best qualified to make them. People are valued and rewarded based on their knowledge, contributions, and their reputations inside and outside the company.

Most are somewhere between these two extremes. Mechanistic organisations usually survive only in market conditions that are stable and predictable. In an unstable, unpredictable, fast-moving market, only an organic organisation will thrive. This also applies to different teams and departments—it is common for both mechanistic and organic structures to exist in the same organisation.

> In an unstable, unpredictable, fast-moving market, only an organic organisation will thrive.

Within the extremes, there are identifiable types. These are not the only ones that exist but they do give a useful feel for the impact of structure on innovation.

- **The simple structure** is organised organically around one person. The good news for innovation is that decisions generate actions very quickly and that you know whom to influence to get your ideas used. The bad news is that everyone is dependent on the opinions and available time of just one person. Bad decisions remain unchallenged. Necessary decisions remain unmade. If the leader has the right qualities, there is nothing better for making breakthrough innovations.

- **The machine bureaucracy** is designed for efficiency. Company growth encourages the hiring of more experienced managers who make more rules to meet the demands of bigger customers and bigger volume sales. Everything is organised like an assembly line. Typically, managers conclude that they don't need new ideas, avoid anything that disturbs efficiency and ignore the ideas of their people. This approach can drive out variation and experimentation. Innovation stops.

- **The professional bureaucracy** is more decentralised because the people it employs have professions that are harder to micro-manage. The problem for innovation is that each profession specialises. These specialities work against the communication and holistic understanding that innovation needs.

- **The divisionalised form** is decentralised *and* organic. The various parts of the organisation are pretty much allowed to make their own decisions. Each focuses on innovating to meet local needs. The result is often that the divisions ignore the centre and each other. This reduces learning and causes missed opportunities.

- **The adhocracy** is highly flexible, designed around projects. The great thing is that they learn and unlearn quickly. This allows them to adapt and innovate rapidly. They find it difficult to maintain their shape and may sleepwalk their way to bureaucracy to find the comfort of specialisation.

While it is good to know the innovation limitations of existing structures, it is even better to design structures to meet your innovation needs. Take the best of the various structures and combine them so that strengths of one approach compensate for the weaknesses of another. There is no one best way.

Take the best of the various structures and combine them so that strengths of one approach compensate for the weaknesses of another.

TRUTH

17

Even useless can be useful

Breakthrough innovation comes from mass experimentation. Trying over and over again to solve stuff from different angles and then rearranging them until something improves. Taking insights gained from useless ideas and using them to generate useful ideas. That's how innovation works.

Expecting all ideas to be useful is unrealistic. It also places unhelpful constraints on creativity. Better to encourage bold playfulness that generates an excess of creativity than to suffocate originality and end up with a shortage.

In an effort to overcome the pressures of practicality, a Japanese author founded an inventor's movement he called Chindôgu—the art of the unusual. There are popular Chindôgu clubs, awards and bestselling Chindôgu books. The rules of Chindôgu formally require an invention to solve a problem while causing so many new problems that they are effectively useless.

Entertainingly useless inventions like a toilet roll fixed to a hat for hay fever sufferers with continually running noses. Plastic cover-all bathing suits for aquaphobics. Wonderful cat-sized duster slippers so the family feline can do its fair share of the housework . . .

The rules of Chindôgu emphasise its philosophy and spirit of anarchy. They cannot be practical. They are not for sale. Nor can they be patented.

These rules appear at first glance to run counter to the notion of innovation as new stuff that is useful. Yet, it's often difficult to distinguish between the results of intentional and accidental Chindôgu—some stuff is designed to have fatal flaws, while other stuff ends up with a fatal flaw despite the best efforts of its designers.

> Some stuff is designed to have fatal flaws, while other stuff ends up with a fatal flaw despite the best efforts of its designers.

Years ago, a scientist at 3M invented a low-tack, reusable adhesive that appeared to be useless. Five years later a colleague of his, who sang in a church choir, used the adhesive to stop his bookmarks falling out of his hymn book. He developed his idea through a series of improvements into the Post-It product that has generated a billion dollars a year for the company. The idea moved from being from being useless to very, very useful.

The 3M story is a reminder that it's not always necessary to start from the beginning when trying to innovate. Start with what exists and just find ways of reducing problems until they no longer exceed the existing benefits. Look around your company. Can you find any examples of accidental Chindôgu?

There is a role for revolutionary change but it's still usually a throw of the dice. You don't know the costs of a new solution until it has been tried. Even if the new idea is fantastic, it will involve adjustment costs. Even if it's brilliant it still risks being implemented poorly in which case its flaws may outweigh its usefulness.

Improve on the useless attempts of others. You will know that someone wants a solution, that others have failed, and what doesn't work. All three are valuable insights when deciding where to put your efforts.

Dr Thomas Starzl, a newly qualified surgeon, took it upon himself to improve upon previous "useless" attempts to perform organ transplants. They were useless because patients just bled to death. So did his first—during surgery. And his second 22 days later. His attempts were termed cannibalisation by his critics. His methods were still, essentially, Chindôgu. Starzl operated relentlessly— sometimes for days at a time. Each operation taught him something. He solved problem after problem with hundreds of breakthrough innovations. Each attempt was a little less "useless". He made remarkable scientific breakthroughs in organ preservation, procurement and immunosuppressants. After four years, he performed the first successful human liver transplant.

There is a link between Chindôgu and the Japanese word for the kind of continuous improvement practised by Starzl. The original kanji characters for Kaizen are KAI meaning "change" and ZEN meaning "good", while the kanji for Chindôgu are CHIN meaning "unusual" and DOGU meaning "tool". Unusual tools create good change.

Unusual tools create good change.

Many attempts to invent produce useless ideas. Many of these useless ideas can become useful given a different situation and enough attempts. Every solution has new problems—and so every new solution requires Kaizen *and* Chindôgu.

18

Every company needs an idea market

People judge ideas too early. The people who judge ideas *before* they are used are not the people who use the ideas. The people who judge ideas are not the people who put the ideas into action. Ideas make it to market not because they have earned the right but because managers have picked them. As a result, they have not endured enough criticism of the right kind. Ideas suffer from insufficient criticism followed by exposure to huge groups of uninvolved users.

You can build a market of ideas that invests resource based on merit, open debate and the passions of the people who will do the work. What should a market of ideas look like?

- **Ordinary genius**—Marketocracy.com, where it turns out that ordinary people can outperform stock markets and brokers by knowing about the value of companies that help them do what they like to do. Markets have been used to predict terrorist attacks, with the Pentagon-sponsored "Policy Analysis Market" (shut down because a couple of senators found it morally repugnant to pay winners), and to predict the failure of companies (luckedcompany.com) with great success. If successful elsewhere, why not use markets to decide the relative merits and resource allocation of your organisation's ideas?

> Why not use markets to decide the relative merits and resource allocation of your organisation's ideas?

- **Reputation management**—eBay.com is the fastest revenue growth company in history. It simply connects buyers and sellers, with the whole process marshalled by a feedback system that allows reputation to be open, vivid and expressed as a percentage. Imagine what would happen if all the people in your company received and gave feedback on their own interactions or on their own ideas? Would Sony have stubbornly ignored MP3 in its digital Walkman if all their 162,000 employees had had a say? One of them must have found the absence frustrating. Someone must have been buying those iPods among so many people!

- **Get what you give**—The open source community operates, broadly, on a get what you give basis. You put more in to get more out. Your reputation and your expertise expand to the extent that your work gains that reputation and expertise. No back-door routes to promotion for people whose only efforts have been to get promoted. It is only in this kind of world that a 16-year-old, Blake Ross, meets a New Zealander online and ends up in charge of an internet browser software project—Firefox— that takes 10 per cent of market share from Microsoft in six months.

- **Waste not, want not**—Wikipedia, a volunteer-created encyclopaedia more popular than britannica.com, has a publicly available section devoted to ideas for improving itself given by readers and enthusiasts. It also has a section full of rejected ideas, with the reasons for their rejection, and an invitation to use the ideas or resubmit. What would happen if Coca-Cola, your government or your company had such a system? Would new ideas be left if it was clear what had worked and what had not yet been attempted?

- **Big brain, little brain**—One of the many ratios calculated to show the effectiveness of an organisation is revenue per employee. Wal-Mart, the world's largest company, has revenues of $174,000 per person but Wal-Mart's frontline employees have no authority or resources to improve profitability via innovation so their only contribution to increasing profitability is in accepting low wages, unpaid overtime and unpaid breaks. What would happen if each employee could invest a proportion of time and money in areas that would assist the company? This would increase the size of Wal-Mart's collective brain and enable it to think, rather than squeeze, its way to more profit.

If people cannot use an idea immediately, they tend to forget it. If you do not store ideas, they disappear. If you do not share ideas, they are wasted. If you do not index ideas, no one will find them.

If you do not share ideas, they are wasted.

A market of ideas gives people a reason to engage in the hard emotional and physical work of getting an idea from ethereal to practical. People will be able to create sufficient wealth to meet their needs and those of their societies.

TRUTH

19

Everyone can learn to think better

Learning to problem solve creatively is not something school teaches us. Creative problem solving is not a subject on many curriculums at kindergarten, college or university. Your people end up without the thinking skills they need. You can learn to think better. Your people can learn to think better.

The brain is a muscle. More accurately, the brain responds to training very much like a muscle. You pump iron and your muscles grow. You exercise your brain and your ability to think grows. It applies to everyone. Anyone who puts in the effort can improve thinking ability. Whether this is the same as innate "intelligence" is not very important at a practical level. What counts is how well someone thinks.

What counts is how well someone thinks.

It's also an untapped resource. You tend to pay for intelligence and achievement when hiring someone. You benefit *only* from that person's ability to solve problems related to your business. Someone can be well qualified and lack the ability to solve problems. They can also be poorly qualified and learn how to solve problems that are valuable to your business.

Evidence shows that teaching people that they *can* improve their thinking *will* improve their thinking. The belief that effort increases practical intelligence encourages that effort. Providing the opportunity to learn how to exercise the brain and the time to practise exercising the brain leads to even greater results.

An experiment with students investigated whether training students to have a growth mindset would improve kids" maths grades. For two hours every week for eight weeks they taught students that brains are like muscles and that everything is hard before it gets easy. They praised effort, *not* intelligence. The brain-is-a-muscle students significantly outperformed their fellow students. Some moved from failure to excellence and sustained that improvement.

Read. Encourage your people to read. Establish a library at home. Use your influence to establish a library or a book club or a book review activity for your team. Many people have *never* read a business book or a biography. Give people personal copies of important titles. More than a third of people do not read *any* books. Read with purpose, make notes, share lessons learned, have authors visit the workplace. It increases what people know and improves their ability to think.

It makes sense to include thinking exercise in your personal routine. Introduce thinking exercise into formal and informal training sessions. Build it into meetings—even routine meetings. Don't save up your creativity exercises for twice a year away-days or occasional brainstorming sessions. Use posters in meeting rooms to list different techniques that remind people to experiment. Support puzzle-solving competitions, games consoles, brainteasers, crosswords and anything else that gets people thinking. This isn't crazy. It's crazy smart. If your people are thinking then they"ll figure out ways of improving what you do and how you do it.

> If your people are thinking then they"ll figure out ways of improving what you do and how you do it.

- Reverse conventional assumptions—What would happen if?
- Reconsider aspects of a product one by one—How can this be different?
- Create mind maps of ideas—How is one idea related to another?
- Explore replacing, combining, adapting, magnifying or reducing something.
- Investigate the forces supporting and resisting an argument or decision.
- Look into the future—What will the world look like? What does it change?
- Expect good ideas—Ask everyone questions until there is a breakthrough.
- Solve problems as a group instead of slavishly ticking off agenda items.
- Imagine yourself as someone or something else to change viewpoint.

As a taster, to give you ten minutes of brain training, here are a few examples. Try them, share them with your team; you"ll find the answers in the back of the book.

1. Can you make eight 8's equal 1000?

2. If you stand on a hard marble floor, how can you drop a raw egg five feet without breaking the shell?

3. After a woman was blindfolded, a man hung up her hat. She walked 50 metres, turned round, and shot a bullet through her hat. How was she able to do this?

4. A man had a flat tyre in front of a psychiatric hospital. While changing tyres he lost four of the five bolts down a sewer. He didn't know what to do until a patient spoke up. What did the patient tell the man to do?

Ask questions. Solve puzzles. Read. Think individually and as a group. Your ability to solve problems creatively sets you apart. This ability can be improved.

TRUTH

20

Find the buzz that works for your people

Innovation is a product of the human mind. It follows that you need to engage the human mind in your efforts to generate innovation. It's about reaching the parts of the mind that other motivators can't reach. It's about stimulating creative urges.

The traditional carrots of promotion and pay don't necessarily work. The people with the ideas aren't all motivated by running in the rat race or scaling the slippery corporate ladder. There are too many people with valuable ideas to promote them all. Similarly, pay is not motivational to everyone. Paying people more money doesn't inspire people to see new possibilities. Paying people more money doesn't encourage sharing, playfulness or imagination. Paying some people more than others can get in the way of the kind of teamwork that you need. Since innovation is necessary for survival, it may not be possible to reward everyone more for keeping the company alive.

It's important to take the time to understand your people. Each of them has something that gets them up in the morning, fills them with hope and puts a smile on their faces. Assuming they are all the same is a mistake. Your industry, company, situation and people vary—so must your motivational approach. One size does not fit all. Find the buzz that works. Let people find the buzz that works for them.

- **Friends and family**—Working with people you like is more motivating than simply keeping a job. People are aware that life is short, that friends are valuable, that family matters. How do you create work that makes life better for the people doing it?

- **Feeling good**—It's how you feel about your work that gives you a buzz. Little things like high quality tools and a comfortable chair. Big things like saving the planet. Work that is more demanding, more important, more worthwhile delivers that feeling of making a difference that people crave. You want work that gives you something to write home and tell your parents about. How do you create work people are proud to do?

- **Creative jobs**—People used to turn up to work and follow

Creativity is valuable but you can't force it out of people.

procedures. Now you want the team to turn up, improve procedures, share knowledge and show initiative! Creativity is valuable but you can't force it out of people. Adding innovation to job descriptions won't add innovation to jobs. Culture matters more than specific jobs. How do you create a culture that welcomes originality? How do you reward initiative by helping people put their ideas into action?

■ **Complexity and trust**—Managers can't understand the detail of everyone's job. They can't track everyone's work. They often don't know where their employees are or what they are doing. They have people inside and outside the company doing or not doing stuff that matters. How do you motivate people you never even see?

The solution? Allow people to redesign their own roles to give them the buzz they need and the innovation you need. This isn't just a once-off exercise. It's something to do fluidly as circumstance requires. Work reflects the needs of the company. Jobs start to fit people in a way they feel uniquely motivating. This is *their* job and they love to do it *their* way.

> Allow people to redesign their own roles to give them the buzz they need and the innovation you need.

Some people build altruism, fundraising or volunteering into their roles. Half of those in the workplace are willing to choose a job based on the opportunity to help others as part of their jobs. Doing whatever they love as part of their work gets their creative juices flowing. It also encourages them to find creative links between the people they want to help and their company. New products, new services and new markets emerge from this desire. One American company created new mobile phone software to allow doctors to track epidemics after an employee recognised an important need while doing voluntary service overseas.

New roles that managers didn't know they needed also emerge. A Brazilian company has an ex-salesman who does nothing but read product manuals for oil wells all day, every day, so that he is ready to advise firefighters after an explosion.

Allow people to innovate with their own motivation. They will start to bring their creativity to work to find new ways of getting the buzz they want and the growth your company needs.

TRUTH

21

Free your children before someone eats them

When you are successful doing one thing, you can be reluctant to do something radically different. It's hard to choose what is radically different if it makes what you do obsolete. It seems wasteful to throw away what works to take a risk on what doesn't. The problem is that if you don't destroy your own business, someone else will.

Evidence shows that companies that are willing to cannibalise their own products, or eat their own children, are more likely to create radical new products. Don't wait for new entrants to find ways of undermining the basis for your business. Don't stick your head in the sand and pretend that it won't happen. It already is.

- **Eating your products**—It's tempting to keep a product around as long as possible. It takes less work in the short term. It's more profitable than launching a new version. You've already paid to design it, build it, market it and distribute it. Why would you want to start again? Three reasons: first, new and improved products stimulate demand. New customers will buy the new product for the first time. Old customers will buy the new version because it's better than the old version. Marketing has a new story to tell. Second, someone somewhere is preparing a product that is radically cheaper or better than your existing product. If you don't replace your own product, someone else will.

  ## If you don't replace your own product, someone else will.

  Traditionally, Ford, GM and Chrysler developed new cars every six or seven years. Japanese competitors started delivering new cars every three years. They created twice as much attention in the marketplace and readjusted designs to suit customer trends twice as often. Twenty years later, GM claim that new product cycles have reduced to three years but Toyota can now develop a new car from design to delivery in only 18 months. It seems like a sacrifice, but by eating their own products they are getting stronger.

- **Eating your market**—It's easy to think that a market will continue for ever. Our customers are happy. Our quality is great. Our profits are fantastic. Everyone needs what we sell. Then suddenly something radically different changes pretty much everything. It solves the problem your product solved but much, much better. The problem your product solved becomes one of many features of the product so that in effect your product is given away free. It meets needs customers didn't even know they had and stops them being interested in the benefits of your product. There is no longer a market for pony express riders, chimney sweeps, canal boats, hieroglyphic writers or gramophone records. The mighty telegraph industry no longer exists. The CD, the DVD, the transistor and the typewriter are all gone. Television may be next.

Someone has probably already sown the seeds of destruction. There are inventors with patents burning holes in their pockets. There are entrepreneurs with ambition burning holes in the parts of the market that don't interest you. There are new entrants who have nothing to defend, no billion-dollar markets, no huge offices, and everything to win by trying.

■ **Freeing your children**—Instead of eating your products or creatively destroying your industry, you can choose to release new ideas into the market. You give these "children" a chance to grow and live with the possibility that they will compete or replace existing products. It's not going to be popular with many managers who will complain that you are making their lives unnecessarily difficult. It's also a challenge to decide when to remain neutral and when to pick a winner.

Honda encourages engineers in its research laboratory to dabble in entrepreneurial, quirky ways. The lab is completely independent from the rest of the organisation. It decides priorities based on what they are curious to discover. It has developed half-a-dozen different products that could kill off gasoline-powered cars, including a fuel cell that produces only water vapour and an air-taxi with engines mounted above the wings.

Many ideas are small enough for existing groups to develop and market them as part of an existing product portfolio—innovation and improvement working side by side. Others only grow big *if* you give them space. They can't always be limited to prototype building or product trials. Some ideas need room to establish billion-dollar markets. Let the children make their own way in the world.

TRUTH

22

Get your ducks in a row

Years ago, Sony tried to sell the world Betamax. Its innovative video recording format was first to market with superior quality to VHS—its chief rival from JVC. After eight years of fierce competition, Sony accepted defeat. Recently, Sony tried to sell the world Blu-Ray. Its chief rival was HD DVD backed by Toshiba and Microsoft. This time, after five years of competition, Sony won. What changed?

People rarely just buy an innovation—they buy everything that goes with the innovation. Usually, they buy a system. They also buy into the future of that system. They judge what other people will buy and what other suppliers will do to support particular products. Unsupported innovation may not be worth buying.

Companies supporting the system also have choices. They choose what is good for them now and in the future. This includes a judgement about what competitors and customers will do. Standing out can be a good thing but being the odd one out is not. Unpopular innovation may not be worth supporting.

Standing out can be a good thing but being the odd one out is not.

In an American bowling alley the skittles, or pins, are known as ducks. They must be lined up in a row to make a strike possible. The success of most innovations depends on getting your ducks in a row. Make sure that all the people *outside* your company who need to support your innovation are lined up and ready to go.

When Sony bought two Hollywood movie studios, it also bought one of the ducks it needed. It was free to provide support for its new Blu-Ray format. It was equally free to withhold support for the rival HD-DVD format. It also had a network of relationships that naturally included other major ducks—the other film studios and the global retailers who decide which format to stock.

Sony got another duck when it entered the games console market. When it launched the latest version, the PlayStation 3, there were already 100 million people who had bought the previous versions. By making the simple decision to include a Blu-Ray player in every new games console it started to outsell standalone HD-DVD players by a ratio of 3 to 1.

Toshiba started the latest format wars at a very significant disadvantage. It didn't have its own games console. It didn't have a movie studio. When people figured that out, the format didn't have a future. Sony was able to influence the expectations about the choices of others regarding which format to support. In this way, it succeeded in coordinating choices based on those expectations.

To make an innovation attractive to customers, they must believe that your innovation will come with a package of support from the market. To make an innovation attractive to players in the market, they must believe that your innovation serves their best interest and most other players in the market will choose it. They must all believe that your innovation has a future.

Getting your ducks in a row is vital. You need to imagine your innovation successfully out in the market. What future are you selling? Which ducks do you need? Who matters most? Who needs to decide to support you and in what order? What influence have you got? What do the other players want? By asking these questions, you can work back from the future to decide what to do now.

Getting your ducks in a row is a game. You take actions based on what you imagine other players will do. Everyone in the game is trying to win by anticipating the actions of other players. In interconnected markets, self-fulfilling prophecies occur. Individuals create the collective future that they have imagined.

> In interconnected markets, self-fulfilling prophecies occur. Individuals create the collective future that they have imagined.

Consider the iPod. Customers buy it because it is beautiful and usable but also because it is connected, available everywhere, with a huge online shop for music, and the biggest, best range of accessories. Apple succeeded in getting all the digital ducks of the media industry to line up to support it.

It did this by telling the best available story about the future of media. It may have been the only coherent story that came backed up with software and hardware. Scared by the steal-and-share approach of Napster and eager not miss the party, everyone signed up. Apple didn't invent any of the components but they continue to get their ducks in a row so that every new product launch is a perfect strike.

The name of the game is replacing one status quo with another that has a place in its heart for your innovation. You want it to change to let in your idea but you don't want it to change again and throw your idea out. At least not until you have a better idea ready to take its place.

TRUTH

23

Got to share more to get more

A worker suggests an idea worth millions to her company. Should her managers keep their promise to give her 10 per cent of the value of the idea *even though* it means paying her $1 million? Or should they keep the money and give her a gesture of appreciation, a gift voucher perhaps, since it's the thought that counts?

It seems simple, but it's amazing how many managers forget that you have to share to get people's best work. Don't expect breakthrough innovations in return for free t-shirts or gift certificates. Recognition has its place but it doesn't pay the mortgage. Some managers are tempted by their inner Scrooge when faced with the reality of passing on the profits. Where the idea is lucrative they may find the prospect of paying subordinates more than senior staff uncomfortable. Resist the temptation and the excuses that go with it.

If you want more, higher-quality ideas then you will have to share more. People you trust to generate innovations are smart enough to want fair returns for their contribution. When the path to shared rights and rewards is not clear people tend to keep their best ideas secret or undeveloped. Others will leave to seek rewards from a new employer or by starting up a new company. The people you should most want to keep are those most likely to leave if they do not receive their fair share. The bold, obsessive entrepreneurs leave first.

> When the path to shared rights and rewards is not clear people tend to keep their best ideas secret or undeveloped.

Different kinds of rewards will lead to different kinds of innovation. Short-term bonuses for managers are rarely a good match to increasing long-term innovation. Short-term financial rewards tend to encourage management behaviour that is unhelpful to the innovation process. The volume of ideas becomes more important than their value.

The purpose of sharing rewards is to encourage more great innovations and the behaviour that goes with it. Good ideas take time and effort. Great innovations demand careful, rigorous, imaginative joining-up of ideas. Incentives need to motivate the right kind of effort. Each stage in the innovation process should have a clear rewards mechanism.

Paying people for submitting suggestions, or introducing prize draws that reward some of those who put forward ideas, may generate more suggestions but will not encourage better ideas. The only reward for the act of submitting an idea should be recognition for having participated *along with* access to support, knowledge and training that can help the individual take the next steps to develop the idea.

Lessons and knowledge gained from attempts to implement an innovation deserve rewards. One pharmaceutical company now gives stock options to those brave enough to conclude that their own research projects will ultimately fail. It does this to encourage fast learning rather than back-covering defensiveness.

You can also try rewarding people by promoting them to the most senior levels based on the impact of ideas. It works for 3M, the Post-it people, who also elevate those who have taken personal risks to sell and implement their ideas. This approach has a number of strengths. The hierarchy becomes not only a meritocracy of past results but also a meritocracy of future growth. This is motivational to other innovation-minded individuals and ensures that the leadership team includes an innovation perspective.

Sharing is mirrored behaviour. We share most with those who share with us. Sharing is risky. Sharing new ideas is a gamble: Will the idea be laughed at? Will time spent developing the idea be wasted? Will credit for the idea be given? Will the idea be stolen? Or ruined? The risks are so high that most people need to know that the upsides of sharing are considerable and that the process for sharing can be trusted before they will actively look for ideas that go beyond their job descriptions and pay grade.

Money is not the only motivation for sharing and developing ideas. Sharing the benefits that come from an idea does not only mean financial benefits. You can share

> Sharing the benefits that come from an idea does not only mean financial benefits.

glory, the thrill of creation, the satisfaction of achievement and the respect of colleagues. They are not directly paying the mortgage either but they are attractive to many people as long as they are real and first-hand.

It's tempting not to share benefits, especially for the super-ambitious who often minimise the contribution of others in their own minds and conversations. Such behaviour is greedy and counterproductive because ultimately it will minimise the discretionary contribution that people make. Better, far better, to share.

TRUTH

24

Hell hath no fury like talent spurned

In 1683, a young man, by the name of Eugene, approached the king of France, a man thought to be his father, to request a commission to become a soldier.

The Sun King, fearful of anyone with half a claim to the throne, and believing that Eugene was too ugly to be a great military leader, refused. Eugene was unproven while Louis was undefeated on land for two decades, with half a million men in his army. Did Eugene's loss really matter?

Eugene's ambition, from the perspective of the monarch, was unimportant, but as a direct result of Louis making it impossible for Eugene to make his name fighting for the French, he was forced to fight in the service of strangers and became a willing combatant against his former king. In short, Eugene wanted to prove himself by defeating the man who had rejected him and his talent. It was a costly mistake. Eugene's military brilliance played a vital role in defeating the French in Bavaria and Belgium, disasters that limited the European expansion of the French empire.

Ironically, Louis had become successful precisely because he was prepared to promote people based on their talent rather than on their bloodline. In the first 20 years of his reign, he had empowered talented people to reorganise his kingdom, encourage culture and reform the army. It was only when his fear and arrogance overrode his judgement that his gift for nurturing talent was neutralised—something that anyone who wishes to lead or is responsible for advising leadership should remember.

Usually these lessons are only learned after the damage has been done, but there is no reason why you cannot prove to be an exception.

Larry Ellison, the founder of Oracle and on a good day the world's fourth richest man, developed similar blind spots to the needs of ambitious talent. After working closely with Tom Siebel for six years he rejected his lieutenant's ideas for software to help sales and service teams. As Fast Company put it "There's something poetic about a rivalry between two people who were once teacher and student. Siebel's eight-year-old company is now the clear leader in its field [. . .] they're fierce competitors, who have a lot in common. Both are control freaks full of hubris who seem to revel in openly insulting each other."

"I hate Tom" was one comment from the charming Mr Ellison who eventually spent billions buying back the upstart company. What would have happened if Siebel's ideas had been adopted and nurtured by Poppa Larry in the first place? He wouldn't have had to play second fiddle for the past decade and he would have been able to supercharge the Siebel idea with the existing customer base, organisation and cash. Both men are rich but could have been more successful together than apart.

Something similar happened when the owners of Palm, the PDA maker, failed to allow its founders creative freedom to expand the capabilities of their then-famous Palm computer. Did they stick around to follow the orders of their supposed masters? Nope. The spurned founders left to found a' new rival, Handspring, which competed with "withering personal computer rivalry" over the next five years until Palm "bought them back" in a deal that, in effect, gave the estranged talent's backers control over 30 per cent of the company.

Unfortunately, this proved to be too late to reverse the decline of Palm as an operating system. In 1998—before the acrimonious divorce—Palm had 80 per cent of the PDA market and was considered by many to have the potential to beat Microsoft. But by the time they kissed and made up, they had less than 50 per cent of the market and were losing money.

The Sun King, Larry Ellison and Palm's owners, 3Com, all made the same mistake of assuming that their servants were interchangeably valuable and that even the most gifted among them would remain subservient. This shared misjudgement cost Louis his European expansion, Oracle applications growth for a decade, and 3Com its hard-won edge over Microsoft.

So what can we learn? To answer the question, consider a completely different way of working with talent: "Edison built a community that was deeply committed to the innovation process. Edison worked most closely with Charles Batchelor, an Englishman whose training as both a mechanic and a draughtsman complemented (and grounded) Edison's more flighty visions. The relationship between them was demonstrated by the agreement to split profits 50–50 for all inventions and to receive stock in all resulting companies."

The strength of Edison was, first, that he recognised the collaborative nature of innovation, second, that he was willing to share wealth, and third, that he gave freedom to his chief collaborator so that he could continue to be fulfilled working with him rather than against him.

Every successful venture has a core team to make it work. Failure to nurture that team's effectiveness and loyalty will jeopardise everything that has been achieved.

> Every successful venture has a core team to make it work.

At Apple, Steve Jobs has a small team, headed up by affable Brit Jonathon Ives, who runs its industrial-design department. This group has been responsible for the design behind the "i-revolution" in Apple's fortunes—the iMac, iPod and iPhone. One report described Ives as "about as obsessive-compulsive as you can be without being hospitalised, and his wild enthusiasm for detail is what gives iPods the aura of sleek, otherworldly perfection that has helped make them the quintessential 21st century accessory".

So ask yourself: What would happen to Apple if Ives left? How good would Sony become if they had the iPod man on board? Would Edison have been remembered as a genius if he had tried to grab all the cash and alienated Batchelor?

The wise company understands that each employee can become many times more valuable than when they were first hired. It also realises that dissidents are necessary to innovation. How are you looking after your talent? Can your people achieve more with you than against you? Are you sure?

> The wise company understands that each employee can become many times more valuable than when they were first hired.

25

Hire for how they learn, not what they know

Microsoft is famous in the hiring world for using brainteasers to identify creative problem solvers as part of its interview process: How would you move Mount Fuji? How would you weigh a jet plane without scales? Which way should the key turn to unlock a car door? How do they make M&Ms? Why are manhole covers round rather than square?

Many other companies have started using similar brainteasers. Some combine brainteasers with stress tests. One Wall Street investment bank begins interviews by brandishing an air pistol and inviting the candidate to play a game of Russian roulette. The idea behind all of the questions is to see how you deal with difficult situations and impossible questions.

Unfortunately, hiring brainteaser champions is not a guarantee that the person is creative or that they will help the company innovate. All it really proves is that the person knows how to deal with a brainteaser in a way that you find acceptable.

They are popular for many reasons. Every company has to make hiring decisions. Popular companies deal with tens of thousands of applications each year. Various, mysterious, pseudo-scientific methods reduce that number before inviting candidates for interview. IQ tests don't measure creativity, although there is correlation between creativity and intelligence.

Tests indicate only an ability to do a test. CVs indicate only what someone says they know and what they say they have done. Interviews seem fatally flawed. Research has shown that people give the job to the same candidate after watching a video of the first two seconds of an interview as interviewers did after spending an hour with the candidate. We stick with our snap judgements.

Far more important than what a person knows is how the person learns. What a person knows matters, you want experts, you want knowledge, but it should be taken as a given. If the person can't do the basics then you shouldn't hire them with the expectation that they can. You need enough people in the company who can make whatever it is that you are trying to sell. The way that people have learned what

Learning new things is at the heart of innovation.

they know and the way they intend learning what they will need to know in the future is the difference between candidates. It's also the difference between companies. Learning new things is at the heart of innovation.

Evidence shows that innovation is a skill people can learn. It helps if candidates have already learned the basics. Asking someone how to design a new product is a better way of finding out their approach to innovation than asking them to fill in an aptitude test. Getting someone to work with existing employees to solve problems is a better way of finding out how they fit into the culture than judging them from across the table.

It also helps if you know how innovation works. If you understand the qualities needed for innovation then you can look for them. Are they curious? Are they obsessive? Are they pragmatic? Are they perfectionists? What products and companies do they admire? Can they take risks? Have they done anything exceptional? Can they communicate unreasonable ideas to a sceptical audience?

When you have sorted for basic skills, you could just close your eyes and pick applications at random. Don't worry about the ones you didn't hire. As the joke goes—no one wants to hire unlucky people . . . The serious point is that if you hire at random you end up with a diverse mix of perspectives rather than a carefully selected demonstration of your prejudices and preferences.

Don't just hire for what they can do now or for what you need doing now. Things will change. Consumer tastes will change. The market will change. And if you have hired people for the future, people who can adapt to the future, or people who are already living for the future, then your company will change too.

> Don't just hire for what they can do now or for what you need doing now.

There are many roles necessary to successful innovation. You don't want to hire half-a-dozen Steve Jobs or a room full of Richard Branson clones. You want people to experiment. You need people to take those experiments and kick the bugs out of them. Someone has to market whatever you build. Someone else has to pull the whole thing together. Each can be individually brilliant but each also has to play their part in holistic, day-to-day, ordinary, extraordinary innovation.

TRUTH

26

How much is the future worth?

All investment is about the future. Sometimes you invest in a future that plays by the same rules as today. Other investment is about a new future that plays by new rules. If you take investment decisions on the new future based on today's rules then you can make big mistakes.

Investment decisions are a tricky business. To make them easier, managers often use tools to help with the financial analysis. The problem with these tools is that they value innovation and non-innovation in the same way. They encourage managers to make unfair demands on returns on investment for internal innovation projects.

Ignoring the future is easier on the brain but it makes investing in the future harder. You don't know what will happen but you must assume that doing nothing new will make things worse. You cannot maintain the status quo so the only way of maintaining *your status* in the future is to make innovation investments now. The question becomes not 'should we invest in innovation?" but "what innovation should we invest in?"

> You don't know what will happen but you must assume that doing nothing new will make things worse.

Estimating the future is guesswork. That's the best we can do. Don't confuse forecasting with foreseeing and place too much faith in the numbers in your business models. Don't avoid questioning your own guesswork and trying to do a better job of describing the future. Don't limit your guesses to only a couple of years into the future. If you do, the costs of innovation will look bigger and the benefits will look smaller than they are likely to be—much like looking through the wrong end of a telescope.

Accepting the future will be different can help free investment thinking. Crazy ideas *will* create mass markets. Bizarre business

> The opposite of what works now may be the new orthodoxy.

models *will* revolutionise industries. Stuff that you reject will come back and haunt you. The opposite of what works now may be the new orthodoxy. You still don't know what will work but investing in a portfolio of radical and incremental innovations is the sensible approach to certain uncertainty.

Short-changing the future occurs when managers compare investments by looking at how much *more* cash is required in addition to spending on existing fixed assets. If the investment uses existing assets then it will appear to cost less and create more profit. If an innovative investment does not use existing assets then it will appear to cost more and create less profit.

You hope that investment in brands, training and equipment will protect you from new competitors. You hope that investment in the old way of doing things will act as a barrier to new entrants. It does. It stops new entrants wanting to do things in the old way, your way. It *doesn't* stop them doing things in a new way.

And if they figure out a new way that works, your investments may act as a barrier to you abandoning your old ways, ways that no longer work. You don't want to write off assets that still function but are no longer competitive, so you delay the decision yet further.

Selling out the future happens when you focus more on short-term results than on the long-term health of the company. Most of this pressure comes from what managers think shareholders want. If you receive incentives based on share price, you tend to make decisions based on raising short-term earnings per share. You can even be tempted to use excess cash to buy back shares instead of investing in innovation. It increases the share price temporarily but does nothing to secure the future of the company. Shareholders start to react to earnings announcements more than to product or strategy announcements.

Thriving in the future means innovation. Many managers are incredibly generous when it comes to setting prices for buying acquisitions to play innovation catch-up or returning money to shareholders to boost the share price and their own incentives. They need to be equally generous when determining how much to invest in innovations that will secure the health of the company in the long term.

Discounted cash flow, net present value, marginal costing and earnings per share often underestimate the necessity for innovation. Use of such techniques can disguise faulty assumptions about the future that prevent companies preparing for it until competitive crisis occurs. Your future deserves better.

TRUTH

27

Ideas are fragile, handle with care

Ever had an idea? Have you experienced that eureka moment? Ever had an idea rejected? Have you ever forgotten an important thought? Have you ever gained insights that might make a difference but given up because the prospect of jumping through corporate hoops was too much effort?

Ideas are fragile. They can mean everything if used or nothing at all if wasted. There are many ways of wasting good ideas even if people do share them. There are also many ways of sending the message that people with good ideas would be wasting their time if they shared them with you.

- **Idea Toxic** is a company where thinking is not welcome and thinkers receive no rewards for their efforts. Culturally there is one best way so that people view new ideas as trouble. There is indifference to finding any better way. There is cynicism born of apathy and negative experiences.

- **Idea Wasteful** is a company where managers treat ideas casually. They think that ideas are simple, easy, not really worth doing anything about. They view creativity as the opposite of productivity. There is often no organised way of dealing with new ideas. There may be an underpowered suggestion scheme or an over-demanding return on investment scheme.

- **Idea Friendly** is a company that welcomes new ideas. It knows that they are valuable. It knows that they are necessary. It has a culture that wants to examine ideas and see how they contribute. There is often an organised way of dealing with new ideas as they arrive. There may even be an approach to managing those ideas through to the market.

- **Idea Hungry** is a company that *seeks* out new ideas. It wants to understand the world better. It wants to make a difference. It is driven by curiosity to question assumptions. People view their expertise as a starting point for contributing to new knowledge rather than as a defence mechanism for keeping facts in neat little boxes. Individuals and their networks challenge boundaries. People see impossible as motivational rather than a constraint.

If someone on the frontline of your organisation has an idea, what happens to it? Often a supervisor decides whether to pass it on or not. The filtering process continues until a small number of ideas arrive at the top. Which ideas get through? Ideas that managers believe are acceptable. These are often not the good ideas. They are unlikely to be the transformational ideas or the ideas that inspire the rest of the company. This kind of filter doesn't give enough ideas a chance. Some companies have suggestion schemes, allowing the idea to bypass the immediate manager. Unfortunately, most of these schemes receive less than half an idea per employee each year.

■ **Idea mismanagement** is anything that you do that wastes ideas. If you don't write down ideas, they just disappear. All that effort creating them produces nothing. All the insight and experience wrapped up in the idea is gone. If you don't develop ideas, they sit on the shelf unused. If you don't test ideas, you don't learn whether the idea was good or bad, too early or too late.

> If you don't develop ideas, they sit on the shelf unused.

■ **Idea management** is what you do to protect and nurture ideas. You store and catalogue ideas so that they can be found when they are needed. You test them so that you know what worked, what didn't, and why. Anyone who finds them gets to build on what you learned. People receive support to develop their ideas so that you don't reject gems just because they're unpolished.

Hierarchy and history conspire to disconnect the part that *thinks* from the part that *does*. When thinking and doing are disconnected, innovation is impossible. Greek philosophers, of the upper island class, conceived of the telescope but were unable to bring it to life because they didn't rub shoulders with the artisans who had the glass-manufacturing ability. Sixteen hundred years later a trio of glass polishers brought the telescope to life. The success of old ideas limits organisations from embracing new ideas. Small groups of

> When thinking and doing are disconnected, innovation is impossible.

people responsible for thinking rely on whatever it was that worked in the past. Ideas, good or bad, come from the top. The rest of the organisation is there to do rather than to think. Fewer and fewer ideas make the journey from the centre of the company to the outside world. Your opportunity is to reverse this trend.

28

Innovate your way out of recession

The best way to deal with a recession is to *innovate your way out* of it. You could just cut back on *everything* but you will also cut back on the very things that can help you to survive and grow. You could just continue to spend as if there was no recession but you will run out of money and waste opportunities to improve the way you innovate.

Spending nothing leaves all the positive moves to your competitors. They can get closer to your customers. They can release next-generation products that establish new markets. They can increase the value of their brands and take advantage of the next wave of growth. Sit still and be left behind—even in a recession. Customers spend longer making choices and looking for increased value from their purchases. They will work harder to buy new and improved. If your product is old and unchanged, they may abandon it.

Continuing as though there was no downturn is a missed opportunity. If you can't really afford such extravagance, you may simply run out of money. If you have deep pockets, you may encourage complacency rather than imaginative, bold solutions. In a crisis, there is a temporary willingness to consider better ways of doing things but you will waste them if the message spreads that there is no need to improve.

> Continuing as though there was no downturn is a missed opportunity.

- ■ **Get rid of what doesn't work.** Unnecessary meetings, forms, procedures and checklists clog corporate arteries. They may even increase in times of uncertainty. To feel in control, managers squeeze their people harder—overloading schedules, undermining efforts to improve. The better way is to build a moderately sized bonfire and work collaboratively to burn red tape.

- ■ **Cut back on what doesn't help.** Eliminating waste is at the heart of continuous improvement efforts. Travel expenses are costly. Help your people make the shift to technology that makes travel less necessary. Cisco has halved travel budgets and used some of the money to install high quality video conferencing facilities. In an upturn, it can either reinstate travel or continue to benefit from the new efficiencies. Forget hiring the Olympic medallist or the Everest mountaineer. Invest money to bring in outsiders who can help, not merely entertain. Re-assess training, offices, stationery, business units.

■ **Engage your people.** One worker complained he lost his job because the company wasn't making money but in 20 years no one had asked him for any ideas to improve the situation. There's never a better time to strengthen working relationships. There's never a better chance to engage employee inventiveness in the causes of cost savings and revenue growth. People have to know that making suggestions will not result in them talking themselves out of a job. Give people the honesty and trust they need. You can cheat but there is a price to pay.

■ **Reach out to customers.** The people who buy your products are also thinking about how best to deal with a recession. Your suggestions and proposals for saving them money will receive more attention than usual. There is an opportunity to build strong relationships in the "heat of battle". A sense of gratitude for solutions will often endure beyond the downturn. Customers will show greater willingness to consider radical solutions. They will be more likely to commit to you for longer than in the carefree atmosphere of a boom.

■ **Question assumption, encourage adventure.** Why can't you deliver a product twice as fast? Why can't a product be twice as economic? Toyota started their hybrid car development during a recession. Can you create a mass market from a luxury or niche product? Apple launched the iPod during a recession. While your competitors are full of fear, uncertainty and doubt, you can introduce innovations that others cannot easily imitate because they question traditions. They may even look foolhardy or silly and avoid attention.

■ **Reward smart thinkers.** Through your efforts to bring people together and identify great ideas, make sure you also identify and reward the smart thinkers. Some people shine

Make sure you identify and reward the smart thinkers.

during difficult times because the answers are not obvious. They find ways of squeezing, stretching and supporting growth. If you ask demanding questions and do not accept compromises, you will eventually unearth the real problem-solving talent in your company.

During a recession, many companies grow. After a recession, some companies grow faster than the competition. This is more likely if they have new products that fit customer needs better, engaged people who creatively collaborate, an absence of unhelpful assumptions and a streamlined business. Innovation is relevant to all these objectives. Every crisis brings opportunity to improve.

TRUTH

29

Innovation can be measured

Some people argue that innovation is impossible to measure. If innovation is not measured it can't be managed. You can't prove to doubters that what you are doing is worthwhile. You won't know whether your efforts to innovate are improving. On the other hand, if you measure the wrong things you will manage the wrong things, reward the wrong behaviour and screw up innovation efforts.

Measuring innovation deserves some thought. Your measurement efforts need to reflect the process and purpose of your innovation efforts. You want to know what is happening, identify new opportunities, let everyone know how to get involved and share how innovation can help. Many attempts to measure fail because they are too complicated, too much effort, and too removed from the way that innovation works.

Patents are a popular but limited measure of innovation. The logic here is that a company will patent its most important innovations and that increasing the number of patents is the same as increasing innovation. If only it were that simple! What about the innovations you can't patent? Patents are not relevant to services. How do you measure the difference in quality or innovation between patents? You combine an old patent with a new business model: are you or the patent owner most innovative?

If your industry generates patentable innovations, measure them. Compare your company to your industry and competitors. Group them by type, originating team, and likely impact on the business. Track where they are used and how they have helped financially and competitively. Evidence shows that they are a good predictor of future new products. Just remember that there is no clear link between patents and financial performance. There's much more involved.

Balanced score cards offer a powerful way of measuring innovation. They follow the idea that measuring anything can only be as good as your understanding of what you are measuring. As your grasp of innovation grows, you are better able to measure what matters.

Describing the way innovation works is a group activity. Managers get involved to learn and agree together. This process of creating a shared view of innovation is valuable. It often results in creative new ways of looking at the nature of the management role in moving from objectives to performance. It challenges assumptions as the group thinks about inputs, processes, outputs and outcomes.

Draw a diagram that shows how you believe that innovation should work in your company. Think about how to measure the performance of the various parts of that innovation flow. Keep the model as simple as possible but no simpler. Compare your model with what is already measured. Some should overlap. Others will be completely new. Your measurements should follow the logical flow of innovation from source to market.

Since everything affects innovation, it's tempting to measure everything. Unless you are all-knowing, and all-seeing, this is a mistake. Too many measurements confuse people. They ignore what is overwhelming. Even worse, they may spend valuable time managing the measurements rather than increasing innovation.

> Too many measurements confuse people.

Measurements will be a mixture of objective stuff that is easy to count, like the number of patents, and subjective stuff which is all about opinion, like the quality of an idea. It is important not to focus on the objective just because it seems straightforward. First, most objective measures require judgement. Second, the most important inputs, processes and outputs *are* subjective.

Every company is different but here are some measures that are always worth counting: How innovative do people think you are? How innovative do people think your managers are? How easy is it to get from idea to market? How many innovations are suggested? Where do ideas come from? How many innovations are being studied? How balanced is the range of ideas? How many get to market? What revenue and profit comes from new products or services?

The innovation model is never finished and the measurement system is never perfect. Innovation is a balancing act. The

> Innovation is a balancing act.

measurement system must help people balance their efforts between competing demands for their time. It should be open for discussion so that it can improve as understanding increases.

TRUTH

30

Innovation is not everywhere

There are two strange facts about globalisation. First, innovation activity is not equally distributed around the world. There are tightly focused hotspots of creative production. Second, innovation is becoming more concentrated in particular places, not less. Is it better to move to a hotspot? Or create one?

If everyone has access to documented knowledge then the creation of original solutions depends on the production of undocumented knowledge. If something isn't written down, it's harder to copy. It can also be difficult to share over long distances. This kind of knowledge is tacit and learned by doing. It's the collection of secrets in people's heads and their way of doing things. Creation and use of such knowledge has a social context. Translation of such knowledge requires understanding of the culture that created it.

> If something isn't written down, it's harder to copy. It can also be difficult to share over long distances.

The big three US car manufacturers have struggled to translate the knowledge surrounding the version of continuous improvement used in Japan. They read books about Toyota, hire ex-Toyota employees, and still the miracles of the Toyota system do not materialise. Yet Toyota has successfully used its system with US employees at more than a dozen US factories. It understands the context in which its system works and can re-create it—competitors find it more difficult.

The physical location of a hotspot is important, but the cultural location of a hotspot is vital. The Indian software industry is physically located in India but culturally located via executives with US degrees and US careers. It started to grow after IBM quit the country in 1978. It has taken 30 years to move from technical support, to low-cost programming, to creating innovative products. It

> The physical location of a hotspot is important, but the cultural location of a hotspot is vital.

illustrates the challenges in replicating the conditions necessary to innovate.

Some national cultures and systems are more effective at innovation. China, Japan, Europe, Korea and the USA account for 75 per cent of all patents. Japan creates 3000 patents per million people. Korea creates over 2500 patents per million. The USA trails in third place with around 700 patents per million. The innovation coming from the mid-range countries like France, the UK or Sweden slips to under 300 patents per million, while the whole 600 million people on the continent of Africa produced only 125 world patents in one year.

Innovation hotspots provide huge advantages. The brightest, best, most ambitious minds gather, attracted by the prospect of working with the brightest, best, most ambitious minds. People informally share breakthroughs before the rest of the world sees the resulting products. They also share their failures and the reasons for them— lessons that the rest of the world doesn't get to see. Everything adapts itself to the needs and nature of innovation for each particular industry. Second place, in another city or country, is a long way behind.

Despite these advantages, there are signs that innovation centres are finding it harder to keep the talent they need. Restrictive immigration policies get in the way. Some centres also grow to a point where they overwhelm their own innovation networks. Opportunities are harder to find as the task of matching idea to funding becomes more difficult. Returning home and starting a new company in a less crowded market becomes more attractive. This reverse brain drain has been slow if occasionally dramatic. It is now speeding up.

Mass-market innovation *can* happen outside of global hotspots but there are conditions and limitations:

■ **Skills and knowledge**—It is not possible to innovate in isolation. You need local people with skills and knowledge that are cutting-edge. You also need enough of them to support growth and promote competition that increases performance.

■ **Culture and know-how**—Skills and knowledge are not enough. You need people working within a collaborative culture with the tacit knowledge that makes the best use of skills. It's why Toyota's training centre in India teaches teens personal grooming and self-improvement along with engineering. It's part of the package.

- **Connections and networks**—Knowledge keeps increasing, approaches to innovation change, while customer needs evolve. Innovators have to ensure that they have major, multiple connections with the people in global hotspots.

- **Mass-market access**—The internet only solves access to mass markets for digital products that can be distributed and sold remotely. For a company to gather the resources it needs for global quality innovation it needs access to mass markets.

TRUTH

31

It's a cultural thing

"We were surprised to find", the GE innovation champion said, "that it's a cultural thing. You can't have a process for everything. Some of this has to be felt, experienced, and embraced. Culturally and individually we have to find ways of making those changes seem necessary. So that people do things differently rather than simply making no mistakes."

Anthropologists and artists have been brought into the company to try to help its hard-working, pedal-to-the-metal management "feel the difference" between innovation and production, to help them find the courage to look stupid and the discipline to find new answers when none have previously existed.

Culture is the sum total of the values, beliefs, assumptions and traditions of the organisation. Culture is established at the time that the company is founded and it develops based on the experiences of the people in the organisation. It is not the same as a neatly typed mission statement and cannot be transformed with half-hearted attempts or superficial declarations.

> Culture is the sum total of the values, beliefs, assumptions and traditions of the organisation.

Cultures that encourage innovation	Cultures that discourage innovation
Emotionally connected	Dispassionately disconnected
Power sharing	Power hoarding
Visionary and forward looking	Tied to routine and past practice
Trusting with minimal rules	Controlling and negative
Positive and highly principled	Highly financially focused
People identify with leaders	Remote managers issue edicts
Customer service obsessed	Performance freaks
Thirst for listening and learning	Excessive denial psychology
Valued people like the company	Best people feel devalued
Decisions are based on merit	Hierarchy slows progress

There are differences in character, rhythm, preferences, traditions, jokes, discipline and priorities between the most successfully innovative organisations and the rest. Turning great insights into practical solutions is the result of what is done *and* the way it is done. Making the transition to an innovation culture is difficult because it doesn't depend on policies or processes in isolation.

We used to get away with treating the world as complicated or "folded together"—parts to be separated from the whole and reduced into simple things we could understand, list and control; relationships reduced to hierarchical organisational charts, roles to bullet-pointed job descriptions, understanding the past to tidy graphs in the company report, preparing for the future replaced by project plans.

This view disguises the messy, interconnected, sometimes grubby, ambiguous reality of getting things done and making things better that has always faced humanity. It avoids the truth—which is that the world is complex, or "woven together". Changes to one part of the organisation will lead to consequences in another.

> Changes to one part of the organisation will lead to consequences in another.

Accepting complexity helps improve your organisation as a *whole*. It reveals the limits of management ability to dictate to their organisations or control the future. It brings humility and a helpful pragmatism. The attention of your organisation can turn to producing conditions that are more likely to produce innovation, survival and growth.

Curiously connecting with the world helps your organisation understand how the world works. You build human relationships of interest and respect with customers, partners, suppliers, departments, universities, anyone and everyone that can help. Managers encourage instant messaging, parties, social networking, and anything else that keeps people exchanging ideas and solving problems together.

Loving diversity produces a high-performing cocktail of individuality and community. Differences are celebrated as an attractive, vital feature of the group. Collaboration benefits from increased levels of trust and from people who feel comfortable in their own skins, styles and status.

Embracing uncertainty encourages the risk taking necessary for progress. It is natural for many people to feel uncomfortable with anything that they haven't tried before. Venturing into the unknown is scary for the majority who need to develop confidence that their first mistake will not be punished and the lessons learned will be worth the pain of failure.

Sharing power is the best cure for indifference. This is not just about the number of managerial layers—flat organisations can also hoard power. It is about getting beyond a master–servant or expert–novice dynamic. Strategy should not be limited to the boardroom. Secrets are unhelpful. Behaviour that shuts one group out and creates cliques disrupts the flow of improvement.

Ditching dogma frees companies from the iron grip of the one best way. There is no perfect off-the-shelf solution for all circumstances. There are principles, there are theories, but everything should be open to question.

Doing what's right allows organisations to deliberately, methodically, even joyously renew themselves. Their cultures deliver competitive advantage. By shortening the cycles of renewal or innovation through experimentation, such a culture naturally replaces its own products and services by finding better alternatives.

Patagonia, the outdoor equipment company, began when its founder forged high quality pitons to climb higher, more difficult cliffs. He kept improving the design not because he was forced to by competition, there was very little, but because he wanted the best possible solution. When he realised the damage caused by his flagship product, he replaced it with specially designed chocks, metal nuts on steel wire, to allow climbers safe support without damaging the rock face.

Of course, it's easier to build these values and behaviours in at the start. It's much more difficult to break with the past and transform culture. Many of those managers who are asked to make innovation happen are part of a tradition that discourages innovation. They resort to dispassionate, controlling, negative, highly financially focused methods to try to encourage everyone else to be creative and collaborative!

Change experiences and people will change their behaviour. Over time this behaviour will become sustainable. You will establish an orthodoxy of the unorthodox, where it is considered normal, praiseworthy and necessary to question the way things are and make improvements—simply because doing the right, smart thing becomes natural. If your culture doesn't have these characteristics you will have to depend on other companies for the innovation you need. So, start from wherever you are and work outwards.

TRUTH

32

Just enough disunity for progress

Valuable innovation is often the product of discord and disagreement. "Stop," cries the innovator, "you're going the wrong way." Someone has to depart from conventional wisdom, however convenient and comforting it is. They need to disagree even if they are wrong.

The Goldilocks theory suggests that you need enough unity but not too much, enough disunity but not too much. Too much agreement and there are no new ideas. Too much disagreement and no one can work together to make the new idea work.

At the national level, this happened in fifteenth-century China when the all-powerful emperor ordered the destruction of its ocean-going ships. Because there was no possibility of disagreement, China quickly lost its technological lead over the rest of the world because it was no longer connected to new ideas. In Europe, disunity meant that ideas rejected in one country could be adopted in another. Famously, Columbus pitched his idea to five European monarchs before finding one to support his proposed voyage to bring unimagined wealth to the continent.

At the organisational level, you have the same friction between stability and progress. There are those who want their experience respected and their fiefdoms secured. There are others attracted to discontinuity because they either want things to be different so they can get ahead or they simply like to see things done better. These improvers have an emotional need to see just how well they can do something. They are vital to progress.

The former CEO of Intel was devoted to the idea of scientific debate. In the technical domain, he believed that the best idea should win and the argument should be robust. He called this approach "constructive confrontation" and it enabled Intel to double the number of transistors on a chip every couple of years. He was far *less willing* to embrace ideas questioning *his* business direction. He sent mixed messages about effective leadership, acted as if they were not mixed, made his mixed messages undiscussable, and made the undiscussability undiscussable. At its best, constructive confrontation allowed open debate that improved solutions. At its worst, it allowed powerful managers to crush the arguments of their underlings while pretending that the interaction was a balanced debate between equals. It was only after he retired that the company was able to open up the discussion about business direction. The new CEO holds more than 100 meetings a year with engineers *but* without their managers. New ideas previously squeezed out, in calls for unity of purpose, are allowing Intel to diversify into mobile phones, health care and wireless communications.

Patience is needed with disagreement. The comfortable level of disunity and unity shifts depending on the work that is being done. Most people expect disagreement early on in a project. Some of this disunity is a group finding out about each other while the rest is the result of alternative ideas conflicting and competing. As a project continues, there is growing impatience with anyone who still argues for different approaches or keeps throwing up dissenting opinions. The rest of the group, or managers who are focused on an image of consensus, attempt to isolate the dissenting voices or simply ignore them.

> The comfortable level of disunity and unity shifts depending on the work that is being done.

The goal unifies. If the goal is flexible enough, big enough, broad enough, it is possible for individuals to disagree while still sharing common objectives. Agreement on vision allows progress to be made that utilises diverse viewpoints as a source of strength. Willingness to embrace the benefits of disagreement is a key characteristic of high-reliability organisations. These are companies that operate in high-risk environments like medicine, nuclear fuel, space travel and policing, but have far fewer accidents or problems. They encourage commitment to the objective of having fewer accidents rather than any particular way of achieving it. Substance is more important than style or saving face.

> Willingness to embrace the benefits of disagreement is a key characteristic of high-reliability organisations.

Politely pretending to agree allows bad decisions and increases frustration between colleagues. Aggressively seeking to win arguments, or defend positions, is damaging. It's better if individuals criticise their own ideas without becoming upset and accept the benefits of open enquiry at all stages of projects and in all circumstances. If everyone feels obliged to *sing from the same hymn sheet* and *drink the same Kool-Aid* the chances of innovation diminish because it requires a departure from sameness. Innovation is about making difference work.

TRUTH

33

Leaders get the innovation they deserve

When the Disney CEO was asked to choose one winner from 12 finalists in an internal competition for new business ideas he responded, "Let's just do them all! Can't a company our size try something every once in a while just because it feels right? What if it does fail? It's still not going to cost as much as one expensive movie script."

He *was* right. Not all the ideas worked but the ones that did transformed Disney from a backwater family favourite to a global entertainment mega-giant. And they all came from existing members of the company in the first three months of CEO Eisner's tenure. He adopted a style that was playful and bold, holding informal staff lunches—not to grill them on numbers and projects but to liberate creativity. He led by example by proposing off-the-wall ideas, and encouraging his team to give him ideas that might embarrass them, to give ideas that went too far.

Leaders set the tone. Maybe you know that already but it's worth repeating. Every little thing you do and say as a leader sends a message about what you want, what you care about, and whether supporting you will be worthwhile.

Leaders set the tone.

Steve Jobs told the team building the Apple Mac computer, "We're here to put a dent in the universe. Otherwise, why even be here?" His words gave the team permission to challenge boundaries. Permission freed them to do amazing work. It provided an audience for innovation. They knew that their leader knew and cared about the difference between mediocre and brilliant, ugly and beautiful.

If the leader focuses on the future people will take more time to prepare for the future. Thinking about the future makes it easier to believe the impossible will be possible. Customers will demand, and competitors will deliver, what is impossible now. Working backwards from the future makes it easier to imagine and play our part.

If the leader focuses on the present people will spend most of their time doing what they can in the present. Thinking about here-and-now tends to trap people in the rules and pressure of the moment. People work hard to make end-of-month goals but don't pay attention to what customers need next year. Imagination and investment must come *before* innovation. It is difficult to imagine progress without time in which to make it and difficult to invest effort in the present without time in which to reap dividends. Innovation is unlikely for those stuck in the short term.

Leaders matter to innovation. The way you think. The way you talk. The way you talk about how you think. People look for signals from their leaders. Signs. Symbols. They may say nothing but notice everything.

Leaders matter to innovation.

Radical innovation depends on leadership. People want to know where they are going and whether the destination is worth the pain of the moment. It is here that the leader's ability to make the future seem desirable and a path to that future seem possible is valuable.

There are many best ways of leading originality. Each would depend on the type of company, the people involved and the kind of innovation desired by the leader. Here are three broad groups of effective innovation leader:

- First, the brash, colourful, look-at-me egomaniac who has mile-high expectations and no sense of what can and can't be achieved. Unrealistic. Impossible. Childish. Argues. Throws tantrums. Never satisfied.

- Second, the quiet, unassuming executive. No flashiness. Making decisions about process and rewards that make innovation easier. They work behind the scenes. They avoid the media. They remove bottlenecks. They are about team. Never arrogant.

  Think of Lou Gerstner arriving as CEO at IBM. The company was failing. He made the decision to keep the company together. He urged the company to fight the competition not each other. He understood that the team could solve its own problems as long as egos did not get in the way. He helped the company to free its creativity. Innovation was the result.

- The third group fits somewhere between the other two! The point is that there are two *ways* of leading innovation. Both work. A combination of the two is probably ideal. Inspirational when necessary, methodical facilitator of human creativity for the rest of the time.

TRUTH

34

Little differences make a big difference

You're looking for that groundbreaking, market-changing new idea that sets you apart from every competitor and rival inside and outside the company.

So where should you start? If You're like many people, you"ll be looking for something big. After all, how can you change the world with a small idea? Well, you can because often the biggest advances come focusing on the littlest things.

Most profitable companies and successful individuals succeed by offering something of value that is unique. When we want to improve, we may fall into the trap of only improving the big things. Yet big innovation—trying to figure out a completely new product or innovative new service that your competitors don't have—is not always the best way to start.

Big innovation is not always the best way to start.

It's very difficult to think of such ideas—although worthwhile. It's very tricky to deliver them and even harder to communicate them despite the potential benefits. The good news is that it's often easier and just as profitable to focus on small innovations that make what we already do—for our customers, our bosses, mothers and lovers—better and different.

Toothbrush maker Oral-B figured out that people didn't know or didn't notice that their toothbrush bristles were so worn away that they were useless. So they created a patented blue dye and put it in the middle bristles so that it faded with use, thus letting the customer know that it's time to buy a new toothbrush. Good for the customer's teeth—and good for Oral-B.

Making it easier to find what you are offering is innovation. Think Facebook, Myspace, Linkedin, Google or MSN maps, GPS systems, console games, 24-hour call centres and mini-outlets close to your customers.

Making it easier to make a choice is innovation. Think online comparison tables that include your key competitors" products even if their prices are lower, or free planning software that helps customers use your service better, like IKEA's kitchen designer.

Making it easier to order and purchase is innovation. Think Amazon's one-click ordering or "my account" services that manage company expenditure like Expedia. So is making it easier to pick up your product, like the low-cost truck rental offered by Brico Depot in France.

What about making receiving a product more fun or more useful? There's packaging that you want to keep, like Apple's, or can reuse, like Nutella's chocolate spread; containers that turn into kitchen ingredient containers; even step-by-step video guides that make product installation a joy, not a curse.

Or you could try making products that are easier to store. One roof-rack company offers a free storage system with each purchase. Nintendo's Wii is the only portable third-generation games console, designed to fit into a small rucksack to share with friends. Pepsi designed plastic bottles to be lighter than Coca-Cola's.

You could even make it easier for people to return your product. A major electrical retailer in the UK has put all receipts on a central database so that customers don't have to keep their own—compare that to the hassle you get at most stores.

Remember, lively brainstorming sessions don't automatically bring these sorts of benefits.

Motivational speeches by Everest climbers or Olympic medalists will not automatically make a difference to what you deliver. The difference will come from focusing creativity on improving any of the hundreds or thousands of aspects of what you offer, avoiding wasted effort and letting you reap the big rewards for noticing the little things that others miss.

35

Look outside for a bigger brain

A few years ago, Proctor & Gamble's CEO set a goal to find 50 per cent of its innovations outside the company. His decision has boosted growth, and doubled its billion-dollar brands and share price. Should you limit yourself to the talent inside your company? Could you get a bigger brain with the talents of millions in the outside world?

Every attempt at innovation is a guess. You start with a problem and try to solve it without knowing what will work. The more attempts made to solve a problem the more likely a solution is to emerge.

This approach was famously described by Edison who said, "I have not failed once [to make the light bulb work]. I have succeeded in proving that those 700 ways will not work. When I have eliminated the ways that will not work, I will find the way that will work."

Less well known is that Edison didn't invent the light bulb. It was designed 50 years before he was born! He saved time by buying patents from *outside* the company and improving upon the various designs, and then moved his research team's attention to developing the other inventions necessary to deliver a working lighting system. The innovation, not the invention, changed the world.

Looking outside allows you to eliminate ways that will not work. It also increases the chances of you finding someone who has found the one way that does work. Not because they are necessarily smarter than you but because they have guessed right. You can now move on to new problems that need solving.

The Proctor and Gamble CEO says that he made up the 50 per cent number because it was just a way of saying that "we don't care where the ideas come from". He understood that innovation does not exist in a vacuum and that the important thing is not the origin of the ideas but their usefulness to the company.

> The important thing is not the origin of the ideas but their usefulness to the company.

There are three main advantages of going outside for ideas:

1. You can quickly benefit from lucky guesses where a successful solution is just a matter of working through the many different possibilities. The solution is not difficult, just time consuming. Being open to the right solution wherever it comes from reduces the time required to solve a simple problem.

2. You can find different approaches to solving difficult problems. Such a problem may require a combination of different skills outside of your experience. It may be that it is only a difficult problem if you lack those skills. For those with the required knowledge it is an easy problem.

3. Working with outsiders brings you solutions for problems you didn't recognise as important. The problem *and* the solution are new to you. Or maybe they match one of your existing solutions to an entirely new problem. The solution is old but the application of that solution is new. They bring opportunities that would have been missed with an insider-only perspective.

Increasing external collaboration *increases* innovation productivity. Research produces more usable ideas. Time to market reduces. The choice is not *between* inside and outside ideas or between internal and external innovators. You will need both. Insiders will have to find outsiders with ideas worth pursuing and then work together to deliver innovative products.

Xerox didn't invent photocopiers. Microsoft didn't invent word processing, spreadsheets, email or windows. Apple didn't invent MP3 players. Hoover didn't invent vacuum cleaners. Amazon didn't invent online shopping. Sony didn't invent games consoles, video recorders or portable cassette players. They brought together outside inventions into innovations that people wanted to buy.

Time saved on basic research and invention can be put to use making improvements. The winning difference between one product and another is usually in the new way existing ideas combine rather than the newness of the technology. Each year, products come more richly packed with ideas. New combinations of existing and new ideas. Doesn't matter where they come from.

TRUTH

36

Madonna knows more than your boss

Madonna is the queen of reinvention. She has sold over 200 million singles, making her the most successful female artist of all time. How has she managed to thrive over two decades while others around her have faded away? What can you learn from her approach to innovation?

Having one hit single is hard work, but no one can be sure what will rock and what will rot. Who would have guessed that three teen mouseketeers, Britney, Justin and Christina from the world of Disney, would dominate the pop charts or that an animated frog would outsell serious muzos Coldplay?

You don't know what will be successful next. You do know it will be *different*. Which means that being the same won't work. Which means that you have to reinvent to stay successful.

> You don't know what will be successful next. You do know it will be *different*.

The first hit is the result of a more-or-less chance series of mutations that produce something that better fits the environment, or appeals to the music-buying public more than the next 180 seconds of licks and hooks. Individual ambition keeps new acts constantly bubbling up. They offer new choices for the constantly evolving musical taste of the buying public. Teens know little about past music and so buy the flavour of the moment.

Constant competition in a changing market means that only an act that can change will maintain its position in the charts. Unfortunately, they often don't know why they have been successful—it just happened that way—so find it hard to modify what they didn't design in the first place.

Even worse, they rarely have time to do any mutating of their own since they are busy with tours, interviews, video shoots and music award ceremonies. There are no "free floating resources" left to find new habits, hooks or fashions.

The same stuff happens with organisations and with our

> Success, particularly big success, makes us think that we have the answers.

individual careers. Success, particularly big success, makes us think that·we have the answers. People just keep doing the thing that has brought them success in the past. We even hire people who fit into our established way of doing things.

It reduces the range of variation, in the genotype of the firm and the phenotype of its members, in the service of efficiency. In other words, we endanger future success by betting on the habits of past success.

Lacking either the time or the humility to consider other options, companies naturally lose their competitive position when the market shifts from beneath it. Structural inertia kills the future of a firm just as surely as three-chord monotony will eventually bring about the demise of a band.

Being very good or even better is not enough. You need to become the hub of new things that are as popular as the old things were. Sure it's a risk—the so-called "liability of newness", but then so is staying the same. You can reduce the risk by understanding how the reinvention queens and kings keep all virgin fresh while building on past success.

Madonna does not work alone. Her reinventions come about by listening to those who are listening to music trends and being credible enough to attract producers who are producing the latest thing. She has the reputation of being good for other people's careers—not just her own.

Nintendo is a king of reinvention. It began in 1889 producing handmade playing cards. It experimented with a range of new ventures, including a taxi company, a "love hotel" chain and instant rice. All but one failed—toy making. While desperately looking for new toy ideas, the CEO noticed an extending arm made and used by a maintenance engineer for his own amusement. The Ultra Hand was a huge success, selling 1.2 million units. Its creator, Yokoi, went on to design the Game Boy selling 200 million units. Reinvention continued with the Wii games console.

Success is not an excuse to stop. It's an opportunity to reinvent.

37

Meeting of minds not
mindless meetings

Many meetings are not dialogues. They do not invite contributions. Their style discourages openness. Their structure does little to capture collective and individual opinions. Many brainstorming sessions follow the form but not the function. You have the flip charts, coloured pens, Post-it notes, tea, coffee and buffet lunch, but where is the collective buzz? Where is the startling exchange of insights?

Don't let the chairperson run the discussion. You might want them to open and close the meeting. In between, they should be getting their hands dirty in the middle of whatever passionate, ridiculous, serious, playful problem solving is happening. The most senior person in the room should shut up at the start and the end. Authority lends disproportionate weight to their opinions and encourages many to speak too much, and with too much certainty. Whoever *is* leading the discussion should be respected, relentless and renegade. The bigger the meeting, or the more important, the greater benefit will come from using a virtuoso facilitator. Spend your money on people, *not* a fancy off-site location.

Spend your money on people, *not* a fancy off-site location.

Beware of the dangers of monologues. Often only one person can talk at a time. This reduces the number of ideas that people can discuss *and* allow everyone else to coast, doing nothing, contributing nothing, not even thinking about the problem. People who talk most can block others from sharing their ideas; people forget what they were going to say or just never get the time to say it. It's also tough to be the only speaker in a big group—many people hold back their ideas because they are afraid of sounding stupid. Just telling people to share crazy ideas is not enough.

Getting people to prepare ideas before a meeting can be worthwhile. Not so that they all take turns to present the ideas—this is deathly dull and ineffective—but so that the people attending have done some thinking. It runs counter to many people's preconceptions but brainstorming is not the objective, it's just a technique. It has very many failings in theory *and* practice. Don't assume that group brainstorming is automatically good or bad. It's not what you do but *how* you do it.

Engage people with problem solving. Pin up principles. Consider what works and what doesn't work. Figure out how to get over the typical problems. Most people get tired very quickly. They run out of ideas. They run out of steam. They start coping instead of contributing. If they get bored, they start to play political games or politely disengage. Email suddenly becomes fascinating. So keep people alert, involved, knowing that the meeting has no fixed shape and that their involvement counts and will be noticed.

Make contributions significant. Take photos of the whiteboard jottings so that what is said matters. Use them as your documents so that time is not wasted writing reports that merely repeat, less colourfully, what has been said. You need a way of structuring and recording what the group contributes, so it doesn't get lost, so that people can see what they have said. It avoids repetition, and allows the group to build idea upon idea, climbing insight upon insight. It should make clear the logic and assumptions that surround their opinions.

Get the knowledge and power in the room. Keep an eye on what supporting information is helpful, what is missing and what is irrelevant. If subjects are put on hold because the right people, authority, facts or figures are not in the room then make sure your cast and props are different for the next meeting. Phone a friendly expert during the meeting if it allows momentum to be maintained. Experience tells us that even a few figurative leaves on the line will derail progress. It's a game that is played.

Avoid projects wherever possible. Problem solving is better as a continuous stream of linked activities than as a series of dislocated, disconnected events. A weakness of projects and project thinking is that they are only appropriate for work that has a clear start and end. The objective becomes reaching the final date with minimal blame rather than contributing improvements. The general company population can barely remember what the grand projects are trying to achieve. The mighty programme manager controls only the progress reports. He or she becomes disconnected from the shifting sands and constantly changing waves inside and outside the company.

Create boss meetings that use formal power and informal kudos to get things done. Many senior managers start ducking meetings as soon as they are able, apart from the meetings with anyone who has more power than they do. It's natural but damaging. Ideally, there should be clear meeting paths and purpose so that the boss is involved in enough detail to understand and often enough so that decisions are made that speed up efforts to innovate. The head of the company that makes the BlackBerry email device makes meetings matter. He holds weekly vision sessions to talk to the various teams from all over the company. He holds regular brainstorming meetings that cover the whole span of diverse subjects that concern the company. The product is centre stage, physically there in the meetings so that it is clear what the link is between sitting around a table and what is delivered to the customer.

Stop believing in the one-size-fits-all meeting—Encourage people to just talk to each other. Have as few regulation-length meetings as possible. Have 60-second meetings.

Encourage people to just talk to each other.

Twenty-minute meetings. Create communal spaces of different sizes with sofas and whiteboards so that colleagues can start a chat without waiting for the next meeting. Some companies have used mobile phones to send out instant meeting invitations. Others use multi-coloured gathering areas or flashing lights to attract attention. Get people out of the office. Get yourself out of a rut. Hang out in an art gallery. Hold your meetings in pubs, clubs, parks, restaurants, ice rinks and amusement arcades. Cover for your team so that they can be doing something less boring and more useful. Block out time during work hours for reading, napping, thinking and just meditating.

The processes in and around the meeting diminish ideas, putting them to one side, ignoring conflict or causing it, leaving out what makes groups valuable. If you are going to spend time and money on getting colleagues and customers together then get it right. There's no such thing as a free meeting, so try to make the best use of the time.

38

Most things will fail, get over it

Extinction is a fact. Failure is commonplace. Ninety-nine per cent of all species and organisations that have ever existed have disappeared. Ninety-nine per cent of all species and organisations that exist will eventually disappear. Once you accept that failure is commonplace, you are better able to succeed now and in the future. You can start with a clearer understanding of innovation reality.

Failure of individual companies is not a bad thing for the economy. Failed experiments by one firm provide lessons and knowledge available to others who will eventually succeed. Failure of the old makes way for the new. Failure of the less competent makes way for the more competent. Failure of the competent often happens only after their efforts have forced the market to innovate.

Similarly, failure of individual products or projects is not a bad thing for a company. The problem comes with particular kinds of failure. If the project or product continues long after most people knew it was doomed. If you don't treat failure as an experiment then you will waste valuable lessons. If you find failure built into company DNA you can't get rid of faulty thinking.

Alessi, an Italian manufacturing company, described as one of the most important factories of Italian design, celebrates failure. It has its own "Museum of Failure" and a coffee-table book full of prototypes that didn't work. It wants to work at the border between what is possible and what is not possible. One step too far towards impossible and customers won't understand it. One step too far towards possible and everyone can produce it. Delivering products that customers love but cannot get anywhere else relies on working at the border. And risking failure.

Learning—Acknowledging the role of failure allows you to look for lessons from other people's experiments rather than writing them off as worthless. The first successful vacuum cleaner, rubber tyre, light bulb, computer, mobile phone and automobile all started as failures. Someone grabbed the lessons from past attempts and succeeded.

Making mistakes can be the quickest way of learning. You can

> Making mistakes can be the quickest way of learning.

find out what doesn't work and can avoid wasting time. You can deliberately do what seems unlikely to work. You may discover a non-obvious way of doing something that sits on the high-profit border. You may gain a greater understanding of what is possible and impossible that guides future efforts.

Coping—No one likes to fail but understanding what failure is and what it means can help. The disappointment of failing still hurts but it doesn't hit so hard that you can't work effectively for weeks or months. Knowing that failing isn't the end allows you to recover quickly and get back in the game. People also find it easier to admit problems. At Genentech, the pharmaceuticals firm, leaders receive incentives to flag up failing projects. Better to compensate people than to let them carry on as long-term drains on cash and resources.

Viewing failure differently depends on company culture. People in low self-esteem cultures conclude there is something wrong with them. They hide from the problem. They seek sympathy, not solutions. High self-esteem allows people to take a problem-solving approach to failure. They assume there is a solution and that they are capable of finding it.

Warning—Past success does not guarantee future success. People tend to praise you for present results that have come about

Past success does not guarantee future success.

because of good decisions in the past. Unfortunately, at the very moment you are enjoying your best results you may be making the decisions that will lead your company to extinction. Believing the praise makes it more likely that you will make the wrong decisions. It encourages unfounded belief that the decisions of the past provide a guide to the future.

Competing—Competition is all about mass experimentation. The good news is that some of your many rivals will fail, providing new opportunities. The bad news is that some of them will succeed, providing new challenges. You need to be able to fail to compete. When Google floated on the stock market, it made this clear to investors: "We will fund projects that have a 10% chance of earning a billion dollars . . . Do not be surprised if we place smaller bets in areas that seem very speculative or even strange." So far, they have placed bets on thousands of ideas including YouTube and a multi-million-dollar competition for the first private journey to the moon. Some will fail; many more will fail, and then succeed.

TRUTH

39

Not all networks are created equal

In life, it's not what you know, it's who you know. For innovation, it's what you know *and* what they know. You need other people's knowledge, influence and resources to innovate successfully. Your networks matter. There are different kinds of networks and they matter in different ways.

Should you get to know a few people really well? Or meet thousands of people whom you hardly know at all? Is it best to be in the centre of a network? Or just take part? You will not be surprised to learn that the answer is not so simple. Effective innovation lies in creative use of many different types of network.

> Effective innovation lies in creative use of many different types of network.

You share strong ties of time and common interest with the people you know best. This can be great for solving problems that require specialised knowledge that you share or simple problems obvious to you both. Talking to the same people will bring you the same information. You will probably spend your time talking about things you *both already know*.

There can also be weak ties. A friend of a friend, an acquaintance, a contact, someone you know of but don't know. These people bring you new opinions, information, tastes and ideas. Not because they are more creative than you are but because they spend most of their time in a network where such things are commonplace. What is new to you is old to them.

Without the new information and new perspectives from weak ties, innovation becomes less likely. Yet, strong ties are vital because it is through them that novel information combines with deep knowledge. You will need both. You can also find ways of filling gaps in your own network to connect yourself to people with the information and resources needed by your innovation efforts.

Some networks and connections form deliberately to solve particular problems or achieve certain goals. Other networks emerge from circumstance and grow as circumstance changes. The person you go to school with becomes your best friend who becomes your business partner. The supplier you buy cheap parts from becomes your collaborator in designing an innovative new product. Your networks are not fixed; they can evolve to contribute in unexpected ways to your efforts to innovate. Staying open to network evolution makes it more probable and more beneficial. You never really know who or what will prove most useful.

The world's biggest, most innovative companies are also the most connected. They are at the centre of networks. They benefit from the weak and strong ties between their people and other groups, companies and networks. Your position in a network provides and constrains opportunities.

Evidence suggests that creating formal ties, or alliances, within networks increases the rate, quality and impact of innovation. The good news is that the more you work at it the more the network helps. Investing time in creating trust, and becoming comfortable with each other, produces greater originality. The closer the groups are the more likely it is that they will collaborate. Where geography is a problem then regular working meetings, socialising instant messaging and web cams all help to remove barriers.

Partnership appears to lead to innovation more often than innovation leads to partnership. This is important: working closely with people who know more than you do and have resources you don't increases your chances of making a breakthrough. Firms with large partners grow faster than those without. This may start with just two collaborators who have a success that attracts more partners. The people in the centre of the network become better at collaborating. The result is a cycle of learning, innovation and network growth.

Networks, often informal, built around common areas of interest form a crucial but often unrecognised part of the innovation process. These networks or "communities of practice" exist outside of formal management

> Networks, often informal, built around common areas of interest form a crucial but often unrecognised part of the innovation process.

control. Their members are often just as committed to the community as they are to their employer. They circulate tips of the trade, information and new ideas, in person and using the internet. Networks can spontaneously gather to solve a problem or support innovation. One of the biggest recent examples is the Linux community which grew around one idea from one man in Finland to become a viable competitor to Microsoft. Similar self-managed behavior is common.

All innovations are delivered by networks. So all innovators *need* networks.

TRUTH
40

Open spaces, open minds

Give them a choice and most people vote for private offices. Put them in an open plan office and they will hide behind the dividers. Remove the dividers and they will hide behind piles of personal junk. Throw out the junk and they will mysteriously relocate to corridors, water coolers and nearby parks. Yet for some innovation tasks, being in the same room is the best solution. Why?

Some tasks are inherently solitary. Others are intrinsically collaborative. And there's a lot of cross-over between these extremes. Collaborative work needs moments of introspection. Creative solitude requires feedback, stimulation and an audience.

Creative solitude requires feedback, stimulation and an audience.

Oobeya is the Japanese word for a big open space. Toyota uses the big open room as a way of bringing together large diverse groups to focus on creating innovative improvements to products. The oobeya is not a replacement for the office. It is not a permanent residence for team members. It is a concept as much as location. It can take place anywhere. The idea is to speed up the creativity process by having one place without interruptions, distance, phone calls or emails. In the oobeya, nothing is taboo. It turns the brainstorming ideal into a physical space. It's an idea at the heart of Toyota's success in building innovation into their cars.

In the typical company, project teams spend very little time together. They tend to spend that time in poorly designed rooms. Tables divide individuals. Notebook computers act as electronic barriers. Meeting agendas create little self-contained packages of time and subject matter. Most attendees daydream while waiting for their turn to speak, knowing that most of their audience's minds will disappear elsewhere. Apathy and disconnection are the result.

Mother—the advertising agency that runs campaigns for Coca-Cola—has its own take on big, open spaces. When the company started, its founders shared a table. As they grew, so did the table. In their new offices, they have created a working space with no internal walls, instead strips of plastic, transparent shelves or chain link fencing divide meeting spaces. In the centre is an enormous, winding table that snakes through the office and gives everyone a place of their own.

Not everything about open spaces has been successful. They are only part of the answer. First, they are specific tools for specific tasks. They work alongside private spaces to make a certain kind of relentless collaboration possible. Second, they require collaborative working skills and attitudes. A closed meeting will still be a closed meeting even in an open room.

A university spent millions on sparkling open-plan office spaces only to find that they conflicted with its academic culture. There have been rows over snooping, noise, and a ban on using telephones. Housing over one hundred people in one room doesn't appear to fit the nature of the work or those doing it.

Environment affects everyone. Constants: ugly working spaces are loathed, beautiful spaces are loved. Half of us have made career decisions based on workplace aesthetics. People want big television screens, pets, cappuccino makers, table football, neck massages and natural air and light. Some of this is frivolous but much more is about our natural insights into our own creativity.

There is a reason that Microsoft has whiteboards in the corridors and park benches in landscaped gardens. There is logic behind Google's and Cisco's efforts to knock down partitions. There is real purpose in Intel creating clusters of armchairs and library-style tables. They know that space influences ability to innovate.

A dogfood factory in Topeka, Kansas paints different sections of buildings in bright colours to provide natural meeting places for teams to compare ideas, thrash out differences and innovate to solve problems. In Hollywood, film industry people are using online games, Xbox live and Second Life, as an electronic space to throw ideas around. Creative agencies provide gaming consoles because they know that the innovation process requires space free from conscious thought.

You need different spaces for different people for different activities. The best working spaces provide choice. Places to stop and

The best working spaces provide choice.

chat. Places for inspiration. Hidden places for work without interruption. People need the freedom to leave the office to find their own places in coffee shops and street markets. Desks are for filling in forms and filing papers—not for creating, thinking, making, learning or collaborating.

TRUTH

41

People judge you first, then your ideas

Your boss doesn't need life complicating. He's under pressure. She's busy. He's got deadlines. She has objectives. Your manager has a family. A schedule. Your boss has a boss. Head honchos who are stressed, busy, hit by deadlines and under pressure to meet objectives. You want them to say "yes" to your idea. But, it's always going to be easier to say "no".

Only about 1 per cent of proposed ideas are ever accepted. Strangers make most of the decisions about whether to develop your insight. People who don't know you can reject your genius concept. They don't know the way you think. They don't care what your idea has cost you in blood, sweat and tears.

They will judge you *first*. It's a mistake to assume otherwise. There are several reasons people judge the messenger before the message. Innovative proposals are uncertain. They are unproven and trying them in the market is the only way of testing them out. Often, the component parts of a breakthrough idea use knowledge at the cutting edge. The person assessing your idea doesn't have the necessary expertise to judge the future because no one does. If they can trust the messenger, they can trust the message.

They will judge you *first*.

- **Workable ideas**—Potential backers want to know whether you can come up with workable ideas. Take the time to think through the obvious weaknesses in your concept and get tough-but-fair reviewers to look at the idea before you pitch. Just as important, they want to know that you are the *kind of person* that they think can come up with workable ideas—and implement them. Is this idea actionable? What can we *do* with this idea? Can this person make this idea work? Your potential supporter may not even understand the details of the idea but if they believe in your ability to deliver the promised benefits then they can proceed. The more radical the idea is the more backers will want the idea proposer to know how to deliver.

- **Desirable stereotypes**—People make assumptions about "good ideas" people. Are you a professional who combines creativity with production know-how? Are you quirky and unpolished, preferring creativity to reality? Or do you appear young, inexperienced and naïve? Each of these stereotypes can convince people to back an idea—they all bring something that is necessary to successful innovation *and* they all encourage the backer to get involved. A professional needs cash and a partner. Quirky people need steady teams. The naïve need experience.

- **Undesirable stereotypes**—People also make assumptions about "bad ideas" people. Are you a lazy dreamer who hasn't grasped the detail or the vision of what the idea needs? Are you a pushover who abandons an idea rather than defend it? Are you a robot who memorises the proposal and cannot answer questions without PowerPoint guidance? Are you an obnoxious, argumentative used-car salesperson who just keeps trying to sell the idea repeatedly without listening or adapting? Are you the charity case who pleads and begs but wants the money that comes from a job, *not* support for a fantastic new idea? Each of these stereotypes gives backers easy ways to say no to taking a risk on a new idea.

- **Likeable collaboration**—Everyone likes to be part of an idea's development. If you want someone to support your idea, share the idea. You need to involve the audience in the creative process.

> If you want someone to support your idea, share the idea.

You can use your knowledge about the idea and the potential backer to get on the same level. Bring the audience into the concept with a mixture of preparation and improvisation, one question and answer at a time. You can present an idea as a story in which the backer is able to imagine the difference your idea will make and naturally start to picture involvement. You can admit a lack of experience and put forward ideas in a way that invites reconsideration of long-held assumptions. Each approach should be sincere; it's about figuring out how you fit into the world of idea pitchers: if you have expertise, don't try to bully people into accepting your concept. If you don't have any experience, don't try to pretend that you do; just share your insight and solution—let them fill in the gaps.

■ **Passion** gets you a long way. Not all the way perhaps but many idea backers have initially supported an idea because of a passionate pitch. If you don't believe in your idea then how do you expect us to believe in your idea? If you don't have passion for your idea then how do we know you will stick with it until it is successful? If you don't feel passionate then ask yourself why. Is your idea good enough? Are you the right person to deliver your ideal?

The way you present your pitch is important but the way you present yourself is vital. Your audience will judge you first, then your idea.

TRUTH

42

Power is originality's best friend

Two groups of Japanese monkeys were introduced to a new taste. In the first group, caramels were given to monkeys low on the status ladder and after 18 months half of the colony had acquired a liking for the new taste. In the second group, the leader was given the new food—wheat—and within just four hours the whole colony was eating it.

Humans also rely on authority for direction and tend to ignore the advice of unknowns. This is particularly true when unknowns introduce new ideas. People find it easier to accept a new idea from a leader than from an outsider. The support of powerful people is vital to promoting your idea and covering your back.

The support of powerful people is vital to promoting your idea and covering your back.

An unknown Sony engineer low on the status ladder secretly designed a groundbreaking computer audio chip for their competitor's new games console. When executives found out, they demanded his head. The engineer was rescued by the leader of the company who made it clear that challenges to orthodoxy were welcome. He allowed the chip to be completed, and supported the development of Sony's own console. Ultimately, Sony launched the PlayStation, selling more than 100 million units. It would not have happened without a powerful supporter backing up an original thinker.

An unknown researcher, working for a modestly sized company in Minnesota, visited a local garage to test out some batches of waterproof sandpaper—his company's latest product. Overhearing workers cursing, he learned that the heavy adhesive tape and butcher paper used to create two-tone effects often damaged the new paint. He headed back to the lab to try to create the world's first specialist masking tape but failed so often that the leader of the company ordered him to drop the project. Yet when the same leader discovered Drew in the lab still secretly working against orders he said nothing to stop him. Encouraged by this tolerant response, but without formal funding, Drew used hundreds of $99 purchase orders to develop the first 3M tape. It also provided the basis of the multi-billion-dollar innovation culture from which tens of thousands of products, including Sellotape and Post-its, have flowed.

Two hundred years ago, a newly qualified doctor used his connections with men of power to change policy and save lives. He convinced the British Navy to give its sailors lemon juice as a cure for scurvy. The cure had been around for centuries but was ignored because the men who had discovered it were unknowns. Without a cure, scurvy caused more deaths at sea than storms, shipwrecks, combat and all other diseases combined. He did not invent the cure but he did gain friends in high places. He persuaded the Admiralty that preventive medicine was the answer to the scourge of scurvy. With the unquestioned support of the Admiral, he was obeyed.

In each example, the hierarchy ignores the innovations of unknown people. The value of their ideas is dismissed because they lack influence and social status. The ideas are saved when the leader lends credibility to their innovations.

> Ideas will fail *with* powerful support but *few* ideas will succeed without it.

The lesson for would-be innovators is clear—every powerful person needs ideas. Most ideas need powerful people to facilitate, legitimise, popularise and even legislate for their adoption. Ideas will fail *with* powerful support but *few* ideas will succeed without it. Originality needs power to overcome the natural, defensive inertia of the status quo.

The lesson for leaders is also clear—innovators need someone to support them. Most innovators are smart, driven people who find it hard to follow rules. This combination needs nurturing—someone to speak for them when needed, someone to coach them on what to say and how to say it, someone to bend the rules, and someone to guide them politically.

TRUTH

43

Quick fixes can lead to great innovations

Most innovation happens because someone wants a better way of doing something that matters to him or her personally. Most individual attempts to innovate are makeshift, quick fixes. They are not ideal but reveal what the user can accept and at least one solution that works.

In India, the CEO of the Tata Corporation noticed people meeting their transportation needs in a dangerous, yet creative way. "I observed families riding on two-wheelers—the father driving the scooter, his young kid standing in front of him, his wife seated behind him holding a little baby."

This kind of wild, improvised quick fix is common enough in Indian culture to have its own name. Jugaad is a Hindi word meaning a "quick-and-dirty work around". Quick fixes that become necessary because of a lack of resources, crazy bureaucracy, or because the existing solution doesn't meet people's needs.

Local Jugaadu, people who are good at quick fixes, build Jugaad cars, wooden carts with engines converted from water pumps. On the bad side, a top speed of 24mph and brakes that fail much of the time. On the good side, there's no road tax and the $1,000 price tag is just within reach even in a country with an average annual wage of $1,700.

The CEO, Ratan Tata, inspired by the Jugaad quick fixes, wanted to build a 'safe, affordable, all-weather form of transport". He announced that his company would design, build and sell a fully functioning modern motor car for only $2,500.

Four years later his company unveiled the world's cheapest motor car, the Tata Nano, complete with four doors, five seats, a 33bhp, 624cc, rear engine, with a price tag that was still only $2,500. Because they were able to see the various Jugaad solutions in practice, the designers made clear-headed decisions not to provide air conditioning, electric windows or power steering, and in a bold demonstration of twenty-first century Jugaad their design uses plastics held together by glue.

Ratan has been able to deliver a people's car for India, more than a century after Henry Ford did so with his Model T and 80 years after Professor Porsche designed the Volkswagen (literally "people's car"): all three aimed at getting the ordinary worker into modern, affordable, personal transport.

Quick fixes point to real customer needs more accurately than focus groups. It provides shortcuts to ideas that have been pre-tested. Sometimes the user-innovator, our Jugaadu, uses unmodified equipment to do innovative things.

Quick fixes point to real customer needs more accurately than focus groups.

Sometimes equipment is customised to do standard things better. All those improvements do something that is useful to the innovator and to others who face the same problems. They are original ideas with a proven market.

Going to the place, hanging with the user-innovators, is what manufacturer-innovators, people who want to benefit from ideas by selling them, should do. This is particularly effective when the user-innovator is jugaading with a product you already sell to create a new spin-off version or a completely new category.

It's what Ray Kroc did to save his business. He had mortgaged his home to buy a milkshake machine franchise with innovative products that did not appear to have a market. It was hard work to sell even one machine to anyone so he was shocked when he found out that a single restaurant had bought eight of his machines!

He flew to California to see for himself. He visited the McDonald brothers" hamburger restaurant and found that they were using his milkshake machines as part of an amazing innovation. They had created the world's first factory-style assembly line for fast food.

Kroc came looking for an opportunity to sell more milkshake machines. He found an opportunity to be part of the fast food innovation of the century. Fifty years later, the expansion he started had more than 31,000 McDonald's restaurants worldwide.

Most successful innovations in your lifetime will start with user-innovators.

Most successful innovations in your lifetime will start with user-innovators. Find them and use their quick-and-dirty Jugaad solutions as basis of new products, new services and new markets.

TRUTH

44

Reinventing the wheel is a good thing

It's easy to think that something is so simple that you couldn't improve it. So unimportant you wouldn't make any money perfecting it. So low tech your intellect would be wasted even thinking about it. So low margin or low volume that your company would never make a dollar, yen or euro. Think that. Be wrong.

Kumho, a Korean tyre maker, keeps reinventing the humble tyre. It did it by altering the tyres" colour so that customers can coordinate their tyres with their vehicle paintwork. It did it with the world's first 32-inch tyres for SUV adornment. And it did it again by creating tyres that produce red smoke inspired by a video of car drifting. The chemists invented a secret compound and, within six months, the tyres were wowing people in drifting competitions.

By paying attention to customer lifestyles, you can create limitless variations of any product. By adjusting details of a product to reflect new tastes and fashions, you can increase profit margins and follow the popularity curve of new trends.

> By paying attention to customer lifestyles, you can create limitless variations of any product.

In the bad old days, Nike organised around product categories: shoes, apparel and equipment. Now, it focuses on sports, tribes and activities. One shoe is for cricket players in India, another for lacrosse players, another for Native American athletes. There are more than 13,000 different products. All Nike sells are reinventions of shoes, sweats, shorts and socks: $16 billion a year and still growing.

Each reinvention involves innovation. Nike's first breakthrough product came by pouring rubber into a waffle iron to make soles that provide better traction. Four of the seven top runners at the 1972 Olympics wore them. It continued to grow with the Air Jordan shoe with its patented system developed by an independent inventor with pressurised gas inside polyurethane heels. Nike labs have created anti-shock plastics for heels and pro-bounce plastics for toes. Its competitors offer shock-reducing springs and computer chips to cushion joints.

Reinvention of the sports shoe is possible to meet the preferences of individual sports, nations, age groups, genders, fashions. The possibilities for reinvention are endlessly extended by advances in material technology (what it is made of) and production technology (how it is made). Adidas, Nike, Reebok and Converse all offer an individualised service that measures your feet in-store and then delivers your made-to-measure shoes within three weeks. In the future, personal 3D photocopiers will digitally measure your feet in the comfort of your own home. This is not some flight of science fiction fantasy—all the technology required already exists. What element of your product could you customise?

Without "low-tech" products, there would be no market for most "high-tech" products. Consumers do not buy material and production technology directly because they offer no direct benefit. They are useful when packaged into products that consumers want. This is the innovation chicken and egg—meeting consumer demand requires better technology while improved technology can produce new products that drive consumer demand. Buyers and sellers of technology have a mutual interest in working out how to offer innovation to consumers.

New markets require reinvention of the same type of product. Heinz, once famous for its 57 varieties, has more than 1,100 products. It sells ketchup in blue, red, green, purple, pink and orange colours. Each time it introduces a new colour its market share increases. Fashion food.

New tastes within the same market also require innovation. A Canadian man reinvented snack food when he created the first high-energy bar for athletes in his kitchen. The company, Powerbar, now has products for warming up, competing and recovery. Scientists mix carbohydrates, vitamins, minerals, fibre and protein in a blend designed to meet the body's needs. Intelligent food.

Gillette reinvented the safety razor in 1895 by making it disposable, transforming the shaving category from a specialist service to a personalised mass-market. It has continued to reinvent in response to innovation, in anticipation of innovation, and to grow the market. It was the first to launch a razor marketed to women, the double-blade razor, pivot point, lubricating strip, spring-loaded blades, micro fins, triple-blades, battery-powered disposable razor, five-blades and rear-trim blade.

The lesson is that you can reinvent any product. Reinvention of one product category often leads to a new category. You can figure out ways to package new technology into products to cater to new tastes and create new markets.

Reinvention of one product category often leads to a new category.

TRUTH

45

Second can be better than first

Johnson & Johnson created "Chux", the first disposable nappy. This first generation managed to sell its radical new product to 1 per cent of parents with small babies.

Proctor & Gamble launched its product "Pampers" 10 years later. This second generation of disposable nappy managed to capture an incredible 95 per cent of the available market. Can second be better than first?

It is unlikely that the first attempt at anything will be the best attempt ever by anyone. This would be like the very first Olympic 100-metre gold medallist setting a world record that is never beaten. The first product proves that something works but it is improbable that it represents the best solution. Better solutions will follow, all of which have a chance of being more popular than the original.

> The first product proves that something works but it is improbable that it represents the best solution.

Only one company can ever launch a product first. Many of these first-place launches fail to make a profitable market. Even those who lead risk being overtaken by second, third or fourth entrants. Chux was the first to market with a disposable nappy; Pampers was the first to create a mass market, while Huggies created a brand that allowed them to dominate the market for 20 years.

The first product is often designed by experts for early adopters. Such products tend to be overpriced and overcomplicated for a mass market. This is because the design is not yet perfected, the early adopters want features that the average consumer does not appreciate, and because the economies of scale have not driven down costs. Apple launched the first touch-screen PDA while Palm launched a much simpler product that created a much bigger market.

Being overpriced and overcomplicated for a mass market is not a problem at the beginning. The problem is that the first person with an idea or the first person to launch a product may focus on the customers they have rather than the customers they need. They may not even realise that there is a mass market for their product because they are so used to selling to a niche market.

Xerox was the first to launch a photocopying machine. It created a multi-billion-dollar company selling photocopiers to a niche market of large corporate customers. This was not a problem. It became so good at selling to a niche market that competitors tried and failed to beat them at their own game. This was not a problem. Canon created a photocopier for small businesses and home-users. It was so successful at producing a copier that was less expensive and less complicated that it captured the mass market *and* significant portions of the niche market. This *was* a problem.

If you are first to market, try thinking like someone who has entered the market second. That's hard because redeveloping a version of your product that is simpler and cheaper runs against the sensibilities of many innovators. They like their bells and whistles. They like high margins. The problem is that the mass market will stay difficult to obtain, and vulnerable to competition if you don't keep finding new ways of competing with your own product.

If you are second, or later, to market, figure out what the market leader does not want to do, what the market does not want to lose, and create a product that can appeal to an even bigger group of customers. No company looks after everyone. On occasion, the first product may require more features to qualify as better value. It may even need specialisation to appeal to niche markets. Do this right and you can look after customers that are of no interest to the mass-market leader.

Most of the time, you"ll find it easier to develop a first-to-market product if it has not succeeded in establishing and consolidating a mass market. The benefits of the brand loyalty and the economies of scale that come from being the original and most popular product are difficult to overcome. Recognise a first-to-market innovation early and you can buy, license, imitate or improve it. Amazon, eBay, Schwab, IBM and Microsoft were not first to

> Innovation is a series of sprints; winning the first does not guarantee that you will win again.

innovate but over time they out-manoeuvred and out-innovated their rivals. They were so successful that most people cannot even remember who was first. Innovation is a series of sprints; winning the first does not guarantee that you will win again.

Being first has advantages but so does arriving second. You will benefit from considering the mistakes and limitations of the first attempt. You will be able to talk to customers and suppliers who have understood some of the attractiveness of the product. You can build on the foundations of the first product.

TRUTH

46

Some ideas are easier to swallow

Some innovations spread quickly. They become commonplace within a few weeks, months or years. Others move more slowly. They take decades to become popular. Many never enjoy widespread use. Most fade into obscurity.

Don't blame the customer. Don't reject the underlying invention. There is a difference between innovation hits and misses. Evidence shows that a handful of key innovation attributes explain

Perception of your innovation determines its adoption levels.

most of that difference. Perception of your innovation determines its adoption levels. Understanding them can help you design your innovation to give it the best chance of delivering its benefits.

- **Relative advantage** is how much better customers think it is than the alternatives. This includes doing nothing. If your idea is better but the difference is not obvious, or better but harder to use, or better but requires effort to learn then it loses adoption speed. Why should anyone bother?

- **Compatibility** is how easily it fits with the life of the customer. Does it fit with their values? Does it make sense in their experience? How acceptable is it? Does it sit comfortably with the way they think and live? If your idea challenges existing beliefs it has to overcome them. People are creatures of habit. They like to buy matching ideas, carpets and curtains.

- **Simplicity** is how easy an idea is to understand and use. People have different tolerances for complexity. Some products are too hard for some people to find useful. They may perceive relative advantage in the functionality of an idea. It may be compatible with their lives. If they can't get their heads around the instruction manual, they will reject the idea. No one likes to spend time feeling stupid. Simplicity sells. Complexity slows.

Simplicity sells. Complexity slows.

- **Trialability** is how easy it is to try before you buy. People may be curious about a better way of doing something but not be convinced. If you make a product available on a trial basis, chances increase that it will become popular. If you design your product to make it easier to try then it will reach more people. If you can get trusted people to test and review your product then it will spread faster.

- **Observability** is how easy it is to see the results of using an innovation. Some results are harder to observe. People like to see before believing in a product. To make an effort, they would prefer the proof of the miracle before an act of faith. If an idea prevents problems or brings its benefits slowly or invisibly, then it will be harder to get people signed up.

Some years ago, two entrepreneurs launched Hotmail. Within 18 months, nearly 10 million people signed up as subscribers. It was one of the fastest product adoptions in history. Why was it so popular, so quickly? It offered *relative advantages* to other email—web-based, usable anywhere, anytime without an internet service provider. It offered *compatible* values of freedom, convenience and anonymity. It offered 1-2-3 *simplicity*—surf to web page, choose an email address, get sending. It offered *trialability*—it was free. It offered *observability*—benefits were obvious and people learned about it from emails sent by friends via hotmail. Today there are more than 300 million Hotmail users.

The hotmail story also illustrates three more characteristics of innovations:

- **Innovation decision**—The fewer people involved in a decision, the quicker the rate of adoption. If groups will use your innovation as groups, try to focus on a small number of decision makers. It's often best for innovative products if individuals can make the decisions for themselves.

- **Communication channels**—In the past, mass media has been the most powerful way of increasing adoption of an innovation. This is still true but communications technology has changed the nature of mass media: it includes the internet, the extensive, energetic blogosphere, and social networking services.

- **Opinion leaders**—The influencers and trendsetters actively use available channels of communication to promote whatever they currently support. If opinion leaders are early adopters of an innovation then it will spread more quickly.

TRUTH

47

Sometimes you have to gamble everything

To cross a river you have to jump. You can't take two steps. Some innovations need all your commitment. Some breakthroughs demand all you have. Any less than everything, and they have no hope of working. All or nothing *is* a tough decision. But it's the only choice for obsessive people who love their ideas.

You've probably heard the FedEx story. Rich student at Yale wrote a paper on the benefits of a national overnight delivery service. Sceptical professor gives the paper a "C". The idea revolutionises the post industry and becomes a multi-billion-dollar corporation. What you may not know is that its founder gambled his $4 million inheritance on his idea. At one point, the company was so desperate for cash that he flew to Las Vegas to play blackjack and wired back his $27,000 winnings.

If FedEx hadn't happened, another company would probably have figured it out. The technology, regulation and customer demand eventually pointed in that direction. However, it wasn't obvious in 1973. FedEx had to build a network and a market at the same time. For the innovation to work, its founder had to gamble everything he had *and* another $80 million from fellow gamblers.

If your innovation requires a network *and* a market, you can gamble enough to make it work. You could just forget about your idea. Alternatively, you can wait in the hope that someone else will take the gamble and that you will be able to come into an existing market in a fast second place.

> If your innovation requires a network *and* a market, you can gamble enough to make it work.

Malcolm McLean was a self-made millionaire who built the second-largest trucking company in the USA. He noticed that dockworkers had to individually load every box into a sling, raise them, lower them, remove the sling, and store them away. He realised that it would be better to use large containers and not open them until the final destination. Regulations meant that McLean could not operate as a trucker *and* a shipping company. Nothing happened with his idea for 20 years until he sold his company for

$25 million and gambled it all on building a system and a market for containers.

Today over 18 million containers make 200 million journeys a year. Hand loading cost $5.86 a ton. Containers cost only 16 cents a ton. The container made it possible for Asia to become the world's workshop and brought customers a previously unimaginable variety of low-cost products from around the world. On the morning of McLean's funeral, container ships around the world blew their whistles in his honour. His gamble had paid off.

For established companies, the biggest gamble is to do nothing.

For established companies, the biggest gamble is to do nothing. Continuing in the same direction is still a choice. Assuming that the future will be the same as the past is still a wager. Why gamble everything on a lack of change? Isn't it more likely that the world will be different?

The new CEO at General Electric (GE) recently gambled billions of dollars on green technologies. Eco-imagination, as he calls it, aims to make healthy profits by solving tough environmental problems. He hasn't bet everything but he *is* spending more on researching alternative fuels than the US government. More importantly, he has gambled by changing the focus and culture of the company. GE people will have to move from a conservative by-the-numbers machine to a creative community focused on breakthrough innovation.

Being one of the first high rollers to place his bets has given GE some valuable advantages. GE is at the centre of the "green is green" corporate fraternity. By just associating itself with environmental innovation, GE will reap benefits as the planet seeks solutions. Leading the charge to greener technologies brings the company valuable, patentable knowledge and difficult-to-copy know-how. It also allows GE to influence emerging standards, policy and public opinion to its advantage. Getting ahead of rivals makes it more attractive to insist on the most demanding emissions and efficiency regulations. It also delivers high-performance products that customers want: a jet engine that saves airlines over $350,000 per plane in annual fuel costs, a hybrid diesel-electric train with 50 per cent lower pollution, a washing machine that uses 75 per cent less energy, roof shingles with inbuilt solar panels, and a super-strong plastic that makes car components 40 per cent lighter.

For GE, FedEx and Malcolm McLean, high stakes gambles bought their places at the table. Their investments were big enough to deliver their innovations. They gambled enough to change the world.

48

Success is an s-shaped curve

The individuals in a social system do not all adopt an innovation at the same time. It would be tedious if they did—imagine the lines at the supermarket! For every new idea or product, some people start using it first and others never do. These groups are important. They don't think the same. They don't need the same information. And they all want something different from your innovation.

Study after study has shown a very similar s-shaped bell curve for successful innovation. You have probably seen it before but that shouldn't stop another look. The importance of the curve is that it gives you an idea of what to expect—which groups to identify, what percentage of total market they represent, their characteristics, and what they want. *If* your innovation spreads then it will probably spread like this.

> The importance of the curve is that it gives you an idea of what to expect

- **The innovation lovers** are the 2.5 per cent of people who embrace new ideas. They are looking for novelty and breakthroughs. They are willing to spend what it takes to have the latest gizmos and gadgets. They have technical expertise to allow them to understand and use experimental products. They are able to cope with innovations that don't work. They play a role in testing your idea, providing an initial market and spreading it outside of your company boundaries.

- **The early adopters** are the 13.5 per cent of people who lead opinion. They are a respected part of the local social system. they're the go-to-guys-and-gals if you want to check before adopting a new idea. They are ahead of the majority but not so far that they leave the majority behind. They show others how to use innovation and take their role seriously. If they use it, the majority concludes that the new idea is ready to use.

- **The early majority** are the 34 per cent of people who follow opinion leaders closely. As a result, they adopt innovations just before the average member of a system or market. They may know about a new idea for a long time before they buy into it. They bring an innovation from minority to mass market. They interact with the late majority and help establish the idea as commonplace.

- **The late majority** are the 34 per cent of people who adopt innovations with some level of scepticism. It is only after nearly half of the people in their group have already started using a new idea that they cautiously adopt it. Sometimes this is due to financial constraints that mean they would rather not risk money on something that may not be necessary.

- **The laggards** are the final 16 per cent. They are the last to adopt an innovation. Some of them may avoid a new idea completely. They base their decisions on the past. They are as suspicious of change as innovators are enthusiastic. They don't go looking for new information and so may only learn very late of the existence of new ideas. Adopting new ideas may involve resources they are not able to risk losing.

This s-shaped curve of innovation adoption is what tends to happen if the approach to communicating new ideas follows traditional patterns. It's easier for inventers to sell to people who love new ideas—they have the resources, the interest and the knowledge to invest in new concepts. The people with the greatest propensity to use innovation receive the most attention from the people who are trying to create mass markets.

The problem is that the innovators are not like the mass market. Ideas for innovators only need to be different to be attractive. Products don't have to be simple because they like complexity. Services don't have to be compatible with prevailing values in the system because they don't share those values. Many innovations stall at this stage because they don't focus on the hardest-to-reach groups. You need to design products for the late majority and the laggards because they are the most demanding

> You need to design products for the late majority and the laggards because they are the most demanding groups.

groups. They want the product to be simple, cheap and obviously better than alternative solution.

The s-shaped curve is useful for internal and external innovation efforts. If you have an idea, it needs to find a market inside your company or network before you can implement it. Thinking about how your colleagues and management fit against the adopter descriptions is a powerful way to start spreading your idea.

TRUTH
49

The ideal design is the simplest design

A company in South America wanted to increase profits. Part of its business was exporting meat to North America in refrigerated cargo planes. The bulky refrigerator units reduced the amount of meat carried so that each journey lost money. The solution? It flew the planes at 25,000 feet so the meat stayed frozen without refrigeration!

The ideal design is the simplest design. The first solution that springs to mind is rarely the simplest, and seldom the best. You start by trying to get your head around the nature of the problem. The obvious parts of the problem get your attention rather than new ways they could fit together. Your mind tends to be constrained by the existing system instead of looking outside it. It's easy to think of improvement as adding something rather than taking something away.

Each attempt at improving an existing solution makes the solution more complicated. It becomes difficult for people to imagine that the next generation of product or service could be anything else. How can it be better if it's simpler?

> Each attempt at improving an existing solution makes the solution more complicated.

Mike Pearce, an architect, figured out a way of building offices in Africa without air-conditioning. He based his design on termite mounds that have to stay at a constant 87 degrees. Termites build tunnels that direct breezes at the base of the mound into chambers of cool, wet mud that flow to the peak. They continually open and close the channels to maintain the temperature. His design used 10 per cent less energy, and saved millions by not buying or using air-conditioning.

There is always a choice. Invent something that is an improvement within an existing system or invent something completely new. Improvement of an existing system seems to be less of a risk. A new invention depends on unproven ideas that may never bring rewards. This is the real innovator's dilemma: Should I take the risk to create something new or just keep making obvious improvements to what exists?

Yet something important has changed the balance of risks. The scale of experimentation has increased so much that breakthroughs are happening, outside the system, with far greater regularity. The level of expectation among customers and investors assumes improvement as normal and builds it into the share price. They reward only breakthroughs. They reward breakthroughs because they are so difficult, because they require guts, and because the chances of getting it right are relatively slim for any one company.

Not so long ago, Toyota asked a team to create a car that would be fuel efficient and environmentally friendly. The choice: Should they design an improved traditional internal combustion engine and gain 50 per cent fuel efficiency? Or deliver a completely new hybrid engine with 100 per cent better fuel economy? They chose the hybrid, launched on time, and the Prius became the first mass-market hybrid vehicle beloved of the great, good, rich and famous.

The example illustrates the choice necessary and the benefits of a simpler design. The car engine is still complex but the redesign of the global system for obtaining fuel and dealing with the consequences is simplified. Toyota now has a 10-year lead on its nearest hybrid rival and the reputation for innovation that it wanted. The world now has a car that delivers performance, fuel economy and less pollution, and reduces reliance on oil-rich, war-torn regions, including the Middle East. With a new design, it is simpler to re-imagine a better automotive system than coping with wars, repairing pollution damage and distributing fuel.

It also illustrates the necessity and benefits of reaching beyond expert comfort zones. The Prius required automotive engineers to work on electrical systems like motors and batteries. Instead of tinkering at the margins of efficiency on the plateau of traditional engines, they have moved to a new learning curve.

This is the benefit of breakthrough innovation. It allows you to achieve more by overcoming contradictions and constraints. In the old system, the performance objectives were impossible; in the new system, the performance objectives are just a starting point for additional improvements. Not all breakthrough innovation has to be

Not all breakthrough innovation has to be big.

big but it is only obvious *after* it succeeds. At which point it opens new doors to yet more possibilities.

TRUTH

50

This is going to hurt

Not everything new is good for you. At least it won't feel that way. Even if it's good for you it won't be good for everyone. Maybe, in time, people will welcome the change but not always. Maybe, in time, people will accept that the new way is a better way but not always. New doesn't always work as hoped.

Even successful innovations, those that become popular and offer clear improvements, can be painful for many. The new way replaces the old way, it requires new skills and new approaches, and it makes what you used to do redundant. It may even make you, the individual worker, redundant. It can make the previously important, irrelevant. It can make the previously profitable, penniless.

■ **People pain** Not everyone embraces innovation. Not everyone should. They don't understand why change is necessary. Maybe it isn't. They don't believe that the new approach will work. Maybe it won't. They believe the old way is better. Maybe it is. They distrust the people selling the change. They fear failure. They know that the change will hurt *even if* it's better over the long term.

Let's face it. Some new ideas are worse than the old ones. Attempts at innovating can be disastrous. The University of Utah bet its reputation on cold

Some new ideas are worse than the old way.

fusion and lost. Marconi bet the whole company on mobile phones and lost. Motorola bet $6 billion on the Iridium satellite phone network and lost. The Chinese state bet $30 billion on the Three Gorges Dam in China and has created an environmental crisis. Being new is not the same as being good.

■ **Necessary pain** Even ideas that work can be painful. Pain does not mean that an idea isn't worthwhile. Innovation is a gamble. No one knows what will work before something new is tried. The dot.com crash appeared to be a waste of money

Innovation is a gamble. No one knows what will work before something new is tried.

but instead it provided the experimentation funds necessary to making significant progress. The advances paid for by the dot.com boomers have made the internet technology we enjoy possible. The Iridium satellite network was sold for only $25 million, a huge loss for Motorola, but a huge boon for the 250,000 scientists, explorers and jet-setters who pay for go-anywhere coverage. Cold fusion may revolutionise energy production. It's impossible to predict.

Some of the pain is just hard work. Most people learn quickly, then slowly, and then stop. Innovators put in the effort to achieve greatness and are willing go beyond existing knowledge at the risk of failure and humiliation. Ten years of relentless practice is necessary before becoming world-class—even the young whiz kids often associated with high-tech innovation develop their skills over a decade or more. At 13 years old, Bill Gates had already gained the programming skills sufficient to debug mainframe computers; by the time he launched Microsoft he had put in more than 10 years of hard work.

■ **Industry pain** Making everything digital has made it easier to send, store and search our literature, art, movies and music. As the publishers feared, digitising has also moved the money away from selling the physical copy. They responded by attacking the people doing the innovating, like Napster for music or SideReel for television. They also attacked the people who enjoyed what the innovators were doing, like suing a grandmother because her grandchild downloaded free music tracks. Has attacking either of these groups worked? No. Sales of physical copies reduce year on year. People don't want them; they have experienced better. They have changed the way they want to interact with their music.

Selling devices to store music and movies has been lucrative— iPod, Vodafone. Selling advertising to show the content free has created billions of dollars—radio, TV, YouTube. Why pay inflated prices for content you can listen to free? Why put up with archaic region protection that stops you watching the latest movies? Why only watch what is in the shops? Forget this talk of piracy costing money. Don't blame consumers. Bollywood now simultaneously releases films directly via DVD, download and online. Instead of complaining about stolen revenues, it has found a way of making money from non-customers while making movies free.

Making money can work if you understand the curve, or the wave, or the shape of the revolution. Spend time figuring out what a disruptive technology offers to customers. It's a smarter use of time than beating them up for daring to try something new that doesn't suit you.

■ **Unnecessary pain** Some innovation pain is the result of mistakes. Some of the pain is the result of the willingness of one group to make painful decisions for other groups. Consider your own pain threshold. How much will you pay to get your idea to work? Then think about the price for other people. The more they share your obsession and your passion, the more they will be willing to pay. Involve people to reduce resistance and increase the likelihood of success. Great innovations come at a price, so make it worth paying.

TRUTH

51

Understand change to make progress

To make improvements you will have to make changes. To make changes you will use your understanding of change. Take the time to consider why change happens, how it starts, continues and stops. It will help you to shape change so that it produces the kind of innovations and improvements you want.

From cradle to grave—It feels natural that organisations would have a life-cycle that mirrors the life, pimples, wrinkles and death that every individual experiences. The simplistic view would be that if you can identify the part of the life-cycle, the appropriate actions are obvious. Just manage effort around what is going to happen anyway. You can mother the child, push the young adult, pamper the middle-aged, ignore the elderly and bury the dead.

One of the problems with this approach is that organisations are made *by* humans *but* differ significantly from their individual members. Some organisational characteristics have typical patterns but these are not fixed. They don't have to die. They regenerate, transform and experience metamorphosis. Change within them depends on ideas, *not* on biological body clocks. They survive as long as they keep finding someone to feed them.

Exactly to plan—Some change happens the way it is intended. Change may bring the benefits that were expected. Believing that it will *always* bring the benefits desired is a mistake. Even if change happens as planned, the benefits may not be as desired. There is a ripple effect, one change leading to several more, some anticipated, others completely unimagined. They cascade outwards like complex family trees so that the destination is rarely clear at the start of the journey.

Change may bring the benefits that were expected. Believing that it will *always* bring the benefits desired is a mistake.

It is easy to become locked into a planned pattern of change. This may happen because efforts to bring about planned change were successful. If it worked so well the first time, why not repeat a winning formula? It may also continue even after failure becomes constant, continual and chronic. Your colleagues become committed to the plan through bias and groupthink. With no one successfully challenging the effectiveness of the plan, the reaction to failure may be to invest more time, resources and effort in trying to make it work. No new thinking—just wasted effort poured into a flawed view of how to achieve objectives.

Them, us and compromise—A lot of change happens because of discontent with the way things are. Usually, someone somewhere is unhappy with what they're getting and wants more. It could be shareholders, customers, your boss, the unions or someone's spoilt children, luxury-loving toy-boy or bling-crazy trophy-wife. Dissatisfaction with the status quo leads the individual to seek satisfaction by changing the situation.

The problem is that one set of desires often conflict with another set of competing desires about what is best. Part of this is opinion, the same goal with different views on how it can be achieved. Part is conflict because a change may be good for someone and bad for someone else, so the goal is the source of disagreement.

Where you have more power than those who disagree, it's likely that the superficial victory will be yours. Just remember that you haven't won the argument. You may need to win the argument to engage imagination, goodwill and talent. Some will actively continue to change your mind, or get your plan reversed. But often, all your comrades and underlings have to do to ruin your shiny new plan is to refuse to believe in it.

Survival of the fattest—There's a view that evolution, or competition, will naturally lead to improvements. That view is wrong. There is no certainty that what survives is fitter, or better, or stronger, or more helpful than what becomes extinct. In times of plenty, the competition changes so that everyone survives, and the worst do best because their behaviour is focused on acquiring more stuff rather than contributing. And not everyone in power can notice the difference.

There *is* a general increase of survival for the species, or company, that is best adapted to its circumstance. But this adaptation may be down to luck. The animal or corporation that survives just happens to have the right combination of size, weight, colour and abilities. Animals don't grow tails, fins or wings deliberately. There was no plan—it just turned out that way. The pattern is very similar for the complex processes that lead to particular organisational designs and decisions. Figuring out which part of success is due to good fortune and which is due to good judgement is difficult, perhaps impossible.

What do you do now? Thinking about how change happens allows you to craft attempts to make things better more effectively. You know better than to over-rely on plans, or life-cycles, and to consider the relative merits of competition and negotiation. Plans do not turn out the way you wanted,

> Change is inevitable, progress is not.

so unexpected results will occur. Good and bad things that were not anticipated will happen, so stay alert to new possibilities that are outside of your original plan. Identify the differences in opinion that drive change in your situation and consider how they can be shaped to allow progress to be made. Use differences to improve decisions and challenge assumptions so that what worked in the past, or has been tried in the past, does not trap you. Use your understanding of change to allow you to make changes.

TRUTH

52

Welcome to the innovation factory

In 1876, Edison moved to a small village 25 miles southwest of New York City. At Menlo Park, he created the world's first research and development laboratory. This was Edison's greatest invention. The greatest invention of the nineteenth century was the invention of the method of invention. Will the greatest innovation of the twenty-first century be the method of innovation?

The pace of innovation is increasing. It's getting faster and more reliable. That doesn't mean that individual companies can rely on innovation to keep them ahead of the competition. It means that they can rely on the competition to keep delivering innovation. The only way to compete is to out-innovate.

The only way to compete is to out-innovate.

BMW has its own company-wide innovation factory. It has six hubs on three continents and claims it is the only car company with innovation management covering every part of development. First, in the research stage the whole network, suppliers, universities and employees, search widely for emerging trends and technologies. Second, specialists assess the suitability of new technologies. Third, engineers adapt technologies to customer requirements and implement them "perfectly" in BMW products.

These three steps provide a good starting point. The search is wide: everyone knows that useful ideas may come from anywhere. The pursuit is relentless and focused: everyone expects that the process *will* produce innovations that contribute to the "perfect driving machine". Application is holistic: innovation councils including representatives from all departments consider the design of the whole car very early in the development process. Innovation is cultural: BMW explicitly demands unconventional thinking and views boundless curiosity as a core skill.

If you want to build an innovation factory, there are many roles to consider. Their influence depends on the level of innovation required. Bear in mind that the more the innovation strays from the traditional expertise of an individual the less influential they will become. Those people who provide links to the outside world make the biggest difference, while too much involvement from a powerful manager can tend to edge choices away from radical and back to conservative. Experienced managers are most likely to choose the past rather than the future.

One reason for choosing the past is fear of the unknown. The future can also make specific skills and experience rooted in the past redundant—leaving some people unsure of how they contribute. Just as important is that the future flows from shifting tastes. Some people are just more in touch with fashion—either because of age, part of the package of generational sensitivities, or because they are perpetually avant-garde.

The innovation factory differs from the invention factory of yesteryear. It wants to do the new, new, radical thing, not the better, better, obvious thing. Why park a car when it can learn to park itself? Why steer when it can learn to drive? Let the car wake you up if You're sleepy and spray negative ions to reduce your stress. Relax while the car adjusts your seat position and mirrors, makes your calls and sends your emails. Feel good about yourself as you switch from petrol to hydrogen power at the flick of a switch. This is not science fiction. Innovation factories at Nissan, Mazda, Jaguar, BMW and Citroen already have these technologies—in production or in prototype. They enjoy making fantasy transportation real.

Nokia's innovation factory assembly line snakes all the way out of the door. It rolls past Indian design students and ethnographers who try to understand how form can follow function. It ripples into the lives of customers, inviting them to create the future together through Nokia Beta Labs and the Nokia Lounge. It is trying to make enough room for its own people to think in new ways. Customer and employee competition entries have led to prototypes and products: phones with self-cleaning nanotechnology, phones as flexible wristbands, and phones to help the elderly stay independent.

In the bad old days, we had technology push from R&D labs to the world via pushy sales people. Then those marketing people began using customer surveys to pull R&D towards particular products. The

The innovation factory is something else— it's a relentless, playful, curious run towards the future.

innovation factory is something else—it's a relentless, playful, curious run towards the future. It's the management of creativity and creativity with management. Fordism replaced by Toyotaism. Most companies want the results of innovation; they may invest in it, but only a minority realise what it means, or what the innovation factory needs.

TRUTH

53

What you know can hurt you

Expertise and experience can get in the way of innovation. If you think you know something then it's hard to be open to learning. If you don't even know why you think something, it's hard to be open to the possibility of being wrong. We gain qualifications in what is already known. We are promoted for what we have already done. The problem is that eventually what you know may be wrong, old-fashioned, out-dated, unhelpful and finally dangerous.

If we didn't base some of what we do on the past then we would waste a lot of time. Imagine being reset every morning, your memories erased of everything after you hit 10 years old. You would spend the entire day just trying to figure out where you fit into the world. Everything you did would seem new, but it wouldn't contribute much because everyone would already know it.

Our heuristic memory, the shortcuts we use to let us know how to react based on what we have learned or done in the past, is useful. But these shortcuts are also flawed. You have picked them up at home, school and work. You have learned them from what people have said, how they have behaved, and what you have read and thought. Your brain recognises patterns and processes them according to various prejudices. Not that they are automatically wrong. They are just pre-judged.

Experts, it is said, know more and more about less and less. That's okay. We need expertise—deep knowledge about narrow subjects. It is a problem when experts know more and more about what *matters* less and less. It is a problem when experts know more and more but care less and less about what people know or think. And it is a problem when experts confuse knowing more with knowing everything or think that the assumptions of their community are the same as knowledge. They defend old positions and attack new approaches.

Intimidating infallibility or pretending you are always right may boost your reputation as an expert but comes with some drawbacks even *if* you are usually right. First, no one will tell when you are wrong. Stalin told his generals that Hitler would never invade Russia so they didn't tell him for three days that German troops had crossed the border. Shooting dissenters didn't help either.

Blinding brilliance from experts can leave them with the last word too often. One medical researcher became an expert and then vowed never to write another word on the subject. He viewed gaining expertise as a journey and becoming an expert at the end of the journey. He has since become an expert again in a new field, retired again, and began his third journey.

He asks, "Is redemption possible for the sins of expertness?" and proposed that "more people could retire from their fields and turn their intelligence, imagination, and methodological acumen to new problem areas where, having shed most of their prestige and with no prior personal pronouncements to defend, they could enjoy the liberty to argue new evidence and ideas on the latter's merits".

Expert novices help to look at problems with fresh perspectives. Stupid questions are often just questions that start without the preconditioning of expertise. Try answering them even if they come from someone who has no right to be asking. Your working assumptions are shortcuts but also constraints. An expert from one subject may easily solve puzzles in another because he or she brings new knowledge. Inviting someone smart enough to understand what you are doing but without the downside of years of indoctrination helps avoid the obviously right solution being applied at the wrong time.

Experiments have shown that novices often make fewer mistakes than experts. Novices think about their answers in new ways and apply the knowledge they have from other areas to the problem at hand. Experts can fall into two main traps: some offer off-the-shelf solutions and approaches that make them feel comfortable because they have used them before. Others find decisions difficult because they can see so many sides of the same issue or situation.

> Experiments have shown that novices often make fewer mistakes than experts.

Exploring opposites is a powerful technique for overcoming the constraints of expertise and tradition. List the key components of an accepted solution and then list the reverse of each component. Then try to make the reverse work. Imagine what you would have to change to support it. Consider what the competition would do as a result. Reverse what is obvious to expert opinion and the result is original.

Obvious	Original
Cinema charged money for people to watch films outside of their homes.	Television showed people films for free inside their homes. Advertisers paid for the films. Customers paid for the televisions.
Car manufacturers sell customers cars. Petrol companies sell customers petrol to put in their cars.	Electric car manufacturers sell customers cars and rent batteries to customers to power their cars. Electricity companies sell electricity to charge the batteries.
Product companies put their merchandise in glossy packaging to make the product look good.	Product companies remove all their packaging so that the company looks environmentally friendly. The product now has to look better because that's what the customer buys.
Health insurance companies help customers to pay for their medical bills. They take guesses at how much everyone will need and then divide the total bill by the number of people and everyone pays a share.	Health insurance companies help customers to improve their health. Customers pay on a sliding scale based on their compliance with a health programme. Customers get healthier and reduce the overall cost of care.

"Trust me, it will never happen" is overconfidence based on the flimsy foundation of past knowledge and wishful thinking. There are thousands of wonderful statements by esteemed experts dismissing future possibilities.

On hearing of attempts at anaesthesia, one surgeon exclaimed:

"The abolishment of pain in surgery is a chimera. It is absurd to go on seeking it . . . Knife and pain are two words in surgery that must forever be associated in the consciousness of the patient." Similarly, the space adviser to the British government declared in 1956 that 'space travel is utter bilge." Experts have declared cars, aeroplanes, home computing, radio, telephones and nuclear power impossible.

Accepted wisdom has proved to be wrong many times in the past, so why wouldn't accepted wisdom be proved wrong in the future? Eventually, what is ambitious and rule changing about a discipline or profession becomes routine, backwards looking, a ticket to prestige and a barrier to progress. As Ustinov once said, "If the world should blow itself up, the last audible voice would be that of an expert saying it can't be done."

TRUTH

54

Who the hell cares where it was built?

You may know the nationality of your car company. Do you know where your car was built? You may know where your computer company is located. Do you know where its components were built? How about your mobile phone? Or your television? Do you know where it was designed? Built? Assembled? Does it matter?

When Boeing was left in the dust by Airbus, it realised it was stuck in the twentieth century. It couldn't invent its way back ahead on its own. It didn't have the expertise. It didn't have the time. So it changed. Instead of sending out 2500 pages of suffocating technical requirements to suppliers, it sent a much more manageable 25 pages of guidance. Instead of controlling every component, it encouraged innovation in every component. Five years later, it was back in front with a five-year technology lead over Airbus.

Suppliers can do what you tell them to do. Or they can do *better* than you *know how* to do. They are the experts in their own field. They have insights that you don't. They are more likely to see the possibility of innovation in the detail of individual parts and components. Keeping a supplier at arm's length prevents them being close enough to see how to contribute. Keeping a supplier on a leash prevents them going far enough to exceed expectations.

Limiting a supplier to an unthinking servant is a mistake.

Limiting a supplier to an unthinking servant is a mistake. Big companies sometimes look down on their suppliers. Often companies with big brands feel superior to their suppliers. Companies from the developed world can sometimes assume that they have the expertise and that their suppliers from emerging markets are just cheap sources of parts. This will not work. The developing world is entirely capable of doing everything from strategy through to manufacture and after-sales care. Attempting to limit their input will only limit your results.

Japanese motorcycle companies expected Chinese suppliers to limit their activities to making parts. They did not expect suppliers to figure out a way of manufacturing complete motorcycles. In the city of Chongqing, suppliers developed a modular approach to manufacturing that allows entrepreneurial assemblers like themselves to create complete motorcycles. As a result, China now produces more than half of the world's motorcycles despite its brands being almost unknown outside of Asia. The Japanese companies have been out-innovated.

In a similar way to Boeing, the Chongqing suppliers are not constrained by detailed specifications and blueprints from a fussy, controlling, slow-moving client. Instead, they agree rough plans and broad characteristics sufficient to allow the modules to work together. Within these parameters, suppliers are free to be as creative as they wish to be—leading to huge advantages. Development is in parallel; no one has to wait for detailed specifications so everyone is able to work at the same time. This speeds up development time, reduces costs, increases the amount of innovation in each new module, and enables assemblers to deliver complete products faster than their more traditional rivals.

Dealing with low incomes and low brand loyalty has forced emerging markets to consider radical solutions. Working without corporate constraints has allowed suppliers to build an eco-system of mutually dependent, openly collaborative inventors and manufacturers. This approach of loose, localised modularisation works for any product: cars, computers, sports equipment and household appliances. It's one of the reasons that companies in emerging markets are buying big western brands in financial difficulty. Add a big brand to an existing modularised network and you have a disruptive innovation.

> Add a big brand to an existing modularised network and you have a disruptive innovation.

The question for big brands is whether to work as part of openly collaborative supplier systems or try to compete using a traditional servant–master approach. Collaboration may disrupt the existing markets for big brands but it keeps them involved as assemblers, distributors or marketers. Collaboration scares some people because they fear suppliers will steal their trade secrets but the bigger risk is to miss learning new trade secrets *from* their suppliers.

Pretending to have control where no control is possible is a self-defeating delusion. Even the biggest corporations are still just part of a much bigger system. They depend on the ingenuity and engagement of millions of non-employees for any success they enjoy. Stereotypes about the type of contribution from a supplier or a supplier location distort this reality. Better to accept what is really happening and earn your place in the larger system.

TRUTH

55

You can't control the waves so learn to surf

The waves of innovation are bigger than any individual, company or nation. They are also more complex. You can create something new but there is no way of being sure who will use it or what they will use it to achieve. The trick is to learn to read the signs and then ride the surf all the way to the shore.

The Polynesians were master navigators who travelled without compasses or sextants. They learned to read the patterns formed by waves. They observed that when waves hit an island some are reflected back while others are deflected but continue on in a modified form. Each navigator used the motion of the canoe to feel the way across the ocean.

Recognising waves is a mixture of history and fashion. There are big waves that roll through society over decades, centuries, even ages. Then there are smaller waves, even ripples that change what is popular and what isn't, and what is possible and what isn't. Each industry has its own waves. Each company affects, and is affected by, waves outside its control but within its influence.

Thinking about big waves deepens understanding about the direction of human preference and progress. One example of this is the communication wave. Humans find communication valuable. Evolution has favoured our ability to talk, to conceptualise and to exchange our opinions with others. Each generation shows interest in methods of improving communication: from cave paintings to the printing press; from messengers running between cities to telecommunication satellites orbiting the planet. If you create a way of connecting people that is better, richer, faster and easier then it will replace the old way or, sometimes, just increase the amount of time spent communicating: from occasional letters to obsessive Facebook.

Surfing waves is a mixture of suppleness and strength. You don't know exactly what is coming so adaptability matters as much, or more, than initial direction. Being fast matters because you only have a limited amount of time to complete each activity before the next wave. You don't have long to complete each improvement and get it to customers. Being bold also matters because you have to attack each new wave with enough strength and the right form to get through it without being killed. Being wiped out occasionally is an intrinsic hazard but dying is to be avoided. It's harder than riding a bike because you can't depend on the road to stay still. It becomes even harder when you have to compete with other people and cope with the additional movement, ripples and waves that they cause. You can't simply look at a map because you are trying to reach uncharted islands.

Data is only available about past waves, so theory is needed to predict future waves. It's not the froth; it's the shape that matters. We place bets on our ability to recognise patterns that give us a hint about what will happen next, or what the world will want next that we can provide.

It's not the froth; it's the shape that matters.

Immersing yourself in the cultural, political and social ripples, currents, waves and storms allows you to navigate better because you will recognise shapes. Surf the most popular and least popular of everything: music, movies, sport, theatre, presidential campaigns, scientific journals, night clubs, clothing, celebrities and technology. Talk to people, watch people, use your own product and use your competitor's product. Travel locally and internationally. Visit new places, make something with your hands, and create a piece of art. Each new experience, particularly if it is *not* a lifelong commitment, will deepen your working understanding of waves.

Individual waves give you choices. You can head towards your original direction, hoping the destination you can feel is somewhere you want to go, or change direction because the wave is good for your particular skills, or because the beauty or challenge of the wave just attracts you. Try moves just to see what happens; forget the big prize and just let go.

Strategy, like surfing, sailing or snowboarding, emerges from the interaction between our choices, those of others, and the environment. Continually adjusting your balance, your direction, your speed and your destination is the best way of surfing waves you can't control.

References

Truth 2

Bergdahl, M. (2006). *What I learned from Sam Walton: how to compete and thrive in a Wal-Mart world.* Hoboken, NJ: John Wiley & Sons.

Boyett, J.H. & Boyett, J.T. (2001). *The guru guide to entrepreneurship: a concise guide to the best ideas from the world's top entrepreneurs.* Hoboken, NJ: John Wiley & Sons.

Pudney, R. (2003). Star Trek strategy. *Business Strategy Review*, Vol. 14, Issue 3, Autumn.

Rowley, L. (2003). *On target: how the world's hottest retailer hit a bull's-eye.* Wiley, 1st edn.

Turner, K.L. (2003). *Kmart's ten deadly sins: how incompetence tainted an American icon.* Hoboken, NJ: John Wiley & Sons.

Walton, S. & Huey, J. (1993). *Sam Walton: made in America.* New York: Bantam.

Truth 3

Grove, A.S. (1999). *Only the paranoid survive: how to exploit the crisis points that challenge every company.* New York: Currency.

Michell, T. (2008). *Samsung Electronics and the struggle for leadership of the electronics industry.* Hoboken, NJ: John Wiley & Sons.

Griffiths, P. (2006). Intel inside. *BusinessWeek*, 6 January.

Kamprad, I. & Torekull. B. (1999). *Leading by design.* New York: HarperCollins.

Lewis, E. (2008). *Great IKEA!: a brand for all the people.* London: Cyan Books.

Truth 4

Nassem, J. (1997). *Naming for power: creating successful names for the business world.* New York: Linkbridge Publishing.

Taylor, N. (2007). *The name of the beast: the process and perils of naming products, companies and brands.* London: Cyan Books.

Rogers, E.M. (2003). *Diffusion of innovations.* New York: Free Press.

Bertini, M., Gourville, J.T. & Ofek, E. (2007). *The branding of next-generation products.* Centre for Marketing Working Paper, No. 007–102, 11 February.

Wheeler, J.A. (2000). *Geons, black holes and quantum foam: a life in physics.* New York: W.W. Norton & Co; new edn.

Truth 5

Martin, R. (2007). *The opposable mind: how successful leaders win through integrative thinking.* Boston, MA: Harvard Business School Press.

Altshuller, G. (1996). *And suddenly the inventor appeared: TRIZ, the theory of inventive problem solving.* Worcester, MA: Technical Innovation Center.

Levinthal, D.A. & March, J.G. (1993). The myopia of learning. *Strategic Management Journal*, Vol. 14, Issue S2, pp. 95–112.

Truth 7

Snyder, N.T. (2003). *Strategic innovation: embedding innovation as a core competency in your organization.* San Francisco: Jossey-Bass Business & Management.

Rosenhead, J. (ed.) (1992). *Rational analysis for a problematic world: problem structuring methods for complexity, uncertainty, and conflict.* Chichester: John Wiley & Sons.

Liker, J.K. (2004). *The Toyota Way: 14 management principles from the world's greatest manufacturer.* New York: McGraw-Hill.

Truth 8

Augsdorfer, P. (2004). Bootlegging and path dependency. *Research Policy*, Vol. 34, Issue 1, February, pp. 1–11.

Knight, K. (1967). A descriptive model of the intra-firm innovation process. *The Journal of Business*, Vol. 40, pp. 478–496.

Olin, T. & Wickenberg, J. (2001). Rule breaking in new product development—crime or necessity? *Creativity and Innovation Management*, Vol. 10, No. 1, pp. 15–25.

Truth 9

Young, J. (2003). *A technique for producing ideas*. New York: McGraw-Hill Professional (originally published in 1965).

Truth 10

Sternberg, R.J. (ed.) (1999). *The handbook of creativity*. Cambridge: Cambridge University Press.

Sternberg, R.J. (ed.) (2007). *The international handbook of creativity*. Cambridge: Cambridge University Press.

Veenhoven, R. (1988). The utility of happiness. *Social Indicators Research*, Vol. 20, No. 4, August, pp. 333–354.

Amabile, T.M. & Collins, M.A. (1999). Motivation and creativity. In R.J. Sternberg (ed.), *The handbook of creativity*. Cambridge: Cambridge University Press.

Truth 11

MacKay, C. (2003, originally published in 1841). *Extraordinary popular delusions and the madness of crowds*. Petersfield, Hants: Harriman House.

Leadbeater, C. (2008). *We-think: the power of mass creativity*. London: Profile Books.

Libert, B. & Spector, J. (2007). *We are smarter than me: how to unleash the power of crowds in your business*, Philadelphia: Wharton School Publishing.

Surowiecki, J. (2005). *The wisdom of crowds: why the many are smarter than the few*, London: Abacus Books.

Tapscott, D. & Williams, A.D. (2007). *Wikinomics: how mass collaboration changes everything*. London: Atlantic Books.

Truth 12

Amabile, T., Hadleym, C.N. & Kramer, S.J. (2002). Creativity Under the Gun. Special Issue on The Innovative Enterprise: Turning Ideas into Profits. *Harvard Business Review*, Vol. 80, No. 8, August, pp. 52–61.

Bourgeois, L.J. III. (1981). On the Measurement of Organizational Slack. *The Academy of Management Review*, Vol. 6, No. 1, pp. 29–39.

DeMarco, T. (2002). *Slack: getting past burnout, busywork, and the myth of total efficiency*. New York: Broadway Books.

Morris, B. (2006). Genentech: Brainiacs with passion for science and contempt for business-speak. *Fortune Magazine*, 20 January.

Nohria, N. & Gulati, R. (1996). Is Slack Good or Bad for Innovation? *The Academy of Management Journal*, Vol. 39, No. 5, pp. 1245–1264.

Quinn, J.B. (1985). Managing innovation: controlled chaos. *Harvard Business Review*, May/June, Vol. 63, Issue 3, pp. 73–84.

Truth 13

Berne, E. (1973). *The games people play: the psychology of human relationships*. Harmondsworth: Penguin.

Seligman, M.E.P. (1975). *Helplessness: on depression, development, and death*. San Francisco: W.H. Freeman.

Seligman, M.E.P. (1990). *Learned optimism*. New York: Knopf. (Reissue edn., 1998, Free Press.)

Truth 14

Kim, W.C. & Mauborgne, R. (2005). *Blue ocean strategy: how to create uncontested market space and make the competition irrelevant*. Boston, MA: Harvard Business School.

Kim, W.C. & Mauborgne, R. (2007). Blue ocean strategy. *Leadership Excellence*, Vol. 24, Issue 9, p. 20.

Truth 15

Ghosn, C. & Ries, P. (2006). *Shift: inside Nissan's historic revival*. New York: Currency.

Hamel, G. (2002). *Leading the revolution*, Boston, MA: Harvard Business School Press.

Magee, D. (2003). *Turnaround: how Carlos Ghosn rescued Nissan*. New York: HarperCollins.

Takahashi, D. (2002). *Opening the Xbox: inside Microsoft's plan to unleash a gaming revolution*. Victoria, BC: Crown Publications.

Truth 16

Lam, A. (2000). Tacit knowledge, organizational learning, societal institutions: an integrated framework. *Organizational Studies*, Vol. 21, No. 3, pp. 487–513.

Truth 17

Deming, W.E. (2000). *Out of the crisis*. Cambridge, MA: MIT Press (reprint of the 1986 edition).

Gundling, E. (1999). *The 3M way to innovation: balancing people and profit*. Tokyo: Kodansha.

Kawakami, K. (2005). *The big Bento box of unuseless Japanese inventions*. New York: W. Norton & Company.

Shigeo, S. (2007). *Kaizen and the art of creative thinking—The scientific thinking mechanism*. Homosassa, FL: PCS Inc.

Starzl, T. (2003). *The puzzle people: memoirs of a transplant surgeon*. Pittsburgh: University of Pittsburgh Press.

Truth 18

Hamel, G. (2000). *Leading the revolution*. Boston, MA: Harvard Business School Press.

Hamel, G. (1999). Bringing Silicon Valley inside. *Harvard Business Review*. Vol. 77, Issue 5, pp. 71–84.

Taylor, W.C. (2006). Here's an idea: let everyone have ideas. *New York Times*.

Truth 19

Dweck, C. (2006). *Mind-set: the new psychology of success*. New York: Random House.

Dweck, C. & Mueller, C.M. (1998). Praise for intelligence can undermine children's motivation and performance. *Journal of Personality and Social Psychology*. Vol. 75, No. 1, pp. 33–52.

Michalko, M. (2006). *Thinker toys*. Berkeley, CA: Ten Speed Press.

Raudsepp, E. (1982). *Brain stretchers*. London: Muller.

Answers:

1. $888 + 88 + 8 + 8 + 8 = 1000$
2. Drop it from six feet and the egg will travel five feet without breaking . . .
3. The man hung the hat on the end of the gun.
4. The patient advised the man to remove one bolt from each of the other wheels and use them.

Truth 20

Amar, A.D. (2004). Motivating knowledge workers to innovate: a model integrating motivation dynamics and antecedents, *European Journal of Innovation Management*, Vol. 7, No. 2, pp. 89–101.

Truth 21

Chandy, R.K. & Tellis, G.J. (1998). Organizing for radical product innovation: the overlooked role of willingness to cannibalize. *Journal of Marketing Research*, Vol. 35, No. 4, pp. 474–487.

Christensen, C. (1997). *The innovator's dilemma: when new technologies cause great firms to fail.* Boston, MA: Harvard Business School Press.

Truth 22

Chakravorti, B. (2003). *The slow pace of fast change.* Boston, MA: Harvard Business School Press.

Liebowitz, S.J. & Margolis, S.E. (1995). Path dependence, lock-In, and history. *Journal of Law, Economics and Organization,* Vol. 11, pp. 205–226.

Truth 24

Butter, A. & Pogue, D. (2002). *Piloting Palm: the inside story of Palm, Handspring and the birth of the billion-dollar handheld industry.* New York: John Wiley.

Grossman, L. (2005). Stevie's little wonder. *Time Magazine.*

Hargadon, A. (2003). *How breakthroughs happen: technology brokering and the pursuit of innovation.* Boston, MA: Harvard Business School Press.

Henderson, N. (2002). *Prince Eugene of Savoy*. Phoenix, NY: Phoenix Press.

Southwick, K. (2003). *Everyone else must fail: the unvarnished truth about Oracle and Larry Ellison*. New York: Crown Business.

Truth 25

Poundstone, W. (2003). *How would you move Mount Fuji? Microsoft's cult of the puzzle—how the world's smartest companies select the most creative thinkers*. New York: Little, Brown & Company.

Truth 26

Anthony, S.D. (2005). Can you spot the early warnings? *Strategy and Innovation*, Vol. 3, No. 2.

Barnett, D.F. (1986). *Up from the ashes: use of the steel minimill in the United States*. Washington, DC: Brookings Institution.

Carter, T. & Ejara, D. (2008). Value innovation management and discounted cash flow, *Management Decision*, Vol. 46, Issue 1, pp. 58–76.

Christensen, C.M. Kaufman, S.P. & Shih, W.C. (2008). Innovation killers: how financial tools destroy your capacity to do new things. *Harvard Business Review*, January.

Kochhar, R. & Pathiban, D. (1996). Institutional investors and firm innovation: a test of competing hypotheses, *Strategic Management Journal*, Vol. 17, No. 1, pp. 73–84.

McGrath, R.G. & MacMillan, I.C. (1995). Discovery based planning. *Harvard Business Review*, July–August.

O'sullivan, M. (2006). Finance and innovation. In J. Fagerberg, D.C. Mowery & R.R. Nelson (eds) *The Oxford handbook of innovation*. Oxford: Oxford University Press, pp. 240–265.

Truth 27

Getz, I. & Robinson, A.G. (2003). Innovation or die: is that a fact? *Creativity and Innovation Management*, Vol. 12, No. 3.

De Dreu, C.K. & West, M.A. (2001). Minority dissent and team innovation: the importance of participation in decision making. *Journal of Applied Psychology*, Vol. 86, No. 6, pp. 1191–1201.

Truth 29

Davila, T., Epstein, M.J. & Shelton, R. (2006). *Making innovation work: how to manage it, measure it, and profit from it.* Philadelphia: Wharton School Publishing.

Smith, K. (2006). Measuring innovation. In Fagerberg et al. (eds.), *The Oxford handbook of innovation.* Oxford: Oxford University Press, pp. 148–177.

Lanjouw, J.O. & Schankerman, M. (2004). Patent quality and research productivity: measuring innovation with multiple indicators. *Economic Journal,* Vol. 114 (495, Apr), pp. 441–465.

Truth 30

Asheim, B.T. & Gertler, M.S. (2006). The geography of innovation. In Fagerberg et al. (eds.), *The Oxford handbook of innovation.* Oxford: Oxford University Press, pp. 291–317.

Bathelt, H., Malmberg, A. & Maskell, P. (2004). Clusters and knowledge: local buzz, global pipelines, and the process of knowledge creation. *Progress in Human Geography,* Vol. 28, No. 1, pp. 31–56.

World Intellectual Property Organization (2007). *WIPO Patent Report: Statistics on Worldwide Patent Activity* (2007 edn.). Geneva: WIPO.

Truth 31

Chouinard, Y. (2005). *Let my people go surfing: the education of a reluctant businessman.* New York: Penguin.

Kanter, R.M. (2006). Innovation: The Classic Traps. *Harvard Business Review,* November.

Mckeown, M. & Whiteley, P. (2002). *Unshrink: yourself—people—business—the world.* Harlow: Pearson.

Menzel, H.C., Krauss, R., Ulijn, J.M. & Weggeman, M. (2006). *Developing characteristics of an intrapreneurship-supportive culture.* Eindhoven Centre for Innovation Studies, The Netherlands.

Williams, W.M. & Yang, L.T. (1999). Organizational creativity. In R.J. Sternberg (ed.), *Handbook of Creativity.* Cambridge: Cambridge University Press.

Truth 32

Argyris, C. (2004). *Reasons and rationalizations: the limits to organizational knowledge.* Oxford: Oxford University Press.

Diamond, J. (1997). *Guns, germs, and steel.* New York: W. W. Norton & Company.

Ford, C. & Sullivan, D.M. (2004). A time for everything: how the timing of novel contributions influences project team outcomes, *Journal of Organizational Behavior*, Vol. 25, pp. 279–292.

Pearce, C.L. & Ensley, M.D. (2004). A reciprocal and longitudinal investigation of the innovation process: the central role of shared vision in product and process innovation teams. *Journal of Organizational Behavior*, Vol. 25, pp. 259–278.

Perrow, C. (1984). *Normal accidents: living with high risk technologies.* New York: Basic Books (Princeton University Press, 1999).

Roberts, K.H. & Bea, R. (2001). When systems fail. *Organizational Dynamics*, Vol. 29, pp. 179–191.

Roberts, K.H., & Bea, R. (2001). Must accidents happen? *Academy of Management Executive*, Vol. 15 (August), pp. 70–79.

Truth 33

Capek, P.G., Frank, S.P., Gerdt, S. & Shields, D. (2005). DA history of IBM's open-source involvement and strategy. *IBM Systems Journal*, Vol. 44, No. 2.

Gerstner, L. (2003). *Who says elephants can't dance?: how I turned around IBM.* New York: HarperCollins.

Stewart, J.B. (2005). *Disney war.* New York: Simon & Schuster.

Yadav, M.S., Prabhu, J.C. & Chandy, R.K. (2007). Managing the future: CEO attention and innovation outcomes. *Journal of Marketing*, Vol. 71 (October), pp. 84–101.

Truth 35

Huston, L. & Sakkab, N. (2006). Connect and develop: inside Procter & Gamble's new model for innovation. *Harvard Business Review*, Vol. 84, No. 3.

Hughes, T.P. (1977). Edison's method. In W.B. Pickett (ed.), *Technology at the turning point.* San Francisco: San Francisco Press Inc., pp. 5–22.

Owen, D. (2004). *Copies in seconds: how a lone inventor and an unknown company created the biggest communication breakthrough since Gutenberg—Chester Carlson and the birth of the Xerox.* New York: Simon & Schuster.

Truth 36

Odum, E.P. (1959). *Fundamentals of ecology,* 2nd edn. Philadelphia: W.B. Saunders Co.

Sheff, D. (1999). *Game over: how Nintendo conquered the world.* Wilton, CT: Cyberactive Media Group.

Taraborrelli, J.R. (2008). *Madonna: an intimate biography.* London: Pan Books.

Truth 37

Furnham, A. (2000). The brainstorming myth. *Business Strategy Review,* Vol. 11, No. 4, pp. 21–28.

Osborn, A.F. (1963). *Applied imagination: principles and procedures of creative problem solving* (3rd revised edn). New York: Charles Scribner's Sons.

Kelly, T. & Littman, J. (2001). *The art of innovation: lessons in creativity from IDEO, America's leading design firm.* New York: HarperCollins.

Truth 38

Hannah, L. (1999). Marshall's "trees" and the global "forest": were "giant redwoods" different? In N.R. Lamoreaux (ed.), *Learning by doing in markets, firms, and countries.* Chicago: University of Chicago Press.

Pierce, J.L., Gardner, D.G., Cummings, L.L. & Dunham, R.B. (1989). Organization-based self-esteem: construct definition, measurement, and validation. *The Academy of Management Journal,* Vol. 32, No. 3, pp. 622–648.

Ormerod, P. (2005). *Why most things fail: evolution, extinction, and economics.* London: Faber & Faber.

Schoemaker, P.J.H. & Gunther, R.E. (2006). The wisdom of deliberate mistakes. *Harvard Business Review*, Vol. 84, Issue 6.

Wylie, I. (2001). Failure is glorious, *Fast Company*, September.

Truth 39

Powell, W.W. & Grodal, S. (2006). Networks of innovation. In Fagerberg et al. (eds.), *The Oxford handbook of innovation*. Oxford: Oxford University Press, pp. 56–85.

Truth 40

Belkin, L. (2007). You won't find me in my office, I"m working. *New York Times*, 13 December.

Mitchell-McCoy, J. & Evans, G.W. (2002). The potential role of the physical environment in fostering creativity. *Creativity Research Journal*, Vol. 14.

Kleiner, A. (1996). *The age of heretics: heroes, outlaws, and the forerunners of corporate change*. New York: Doubleday.

Truth 41

Elsbach, K.D. (2003). How to pitch a brilliant idea. *Harvard Business Review*, Vol. 81, Issue 9, pp. 117–123.

Elsvbach, K.D. & Kramer, R.M. (2003). Assessing creativity in Hollywood pitch meetings: evidence for a dual-process model of creativity. *Academy of Management Journal*, Vol. 46, Issue 3, pp. 283–301.

Getz, I. & Robinson, A.G. (2003). Innovate or die: is that a fact? *Creativity and Innovation Management*, Vol. 12, Issue 3, pp. 130–136.

McKee, R. (2003). Storytelling that moves people. *Harvard Business Review*, Vol. 81, Issue 6, pp. 51–55.

Sternberg, R.J. (2002). *Cognitive psychology*, 3rd edn. Belmont, CA: Wadsworth Publishing.

Truth 42

Brown, S. (2004). *Scurvy: how a surgeon, a mariner, and a gentleman solved the greatest medical mystery of the age of sail*. New York: Thomas Dunne Books.

Fahey, R. (2007). Farewell, Father. Eurogamer.net

Truth 43

Von Hippel, E. (1988). *The sources of innovation.* Oxford: Oxford University Press.

Truth 44

Burke, M. (2008). On the run. *Forbes Magazine,* 2 November.

McGibben, D. (1998). *Cutting edge: Gillette's journey to global leadership.* Boston, MA: Harvard Business Press.

von Tunzelmann, N.V. & Acha, V. (2006). Innovation in "low tech" industries. In *The Oxford handbook of innovation.* Oxford: Oxford University Press, pp. 407–432.

Truth 45

Markides, C.C. & Geroski, P.A. (2005). *Fast second: how smart companies bypass radical innovation to enter and dominate new markets.* San Francisco: Jossey-Bass.

Truth 46

Bronson, P. (2000). *The nudist on the late shift and other tales of Silicon Valley.* London: Vintage; New edn.

Rogers, E. (2003). *Diffusion of innovations,* 5th edn. New York: Free Press.

Truth 47

Cudahy, B.J. (2006,). *Box boats: how container ships changed the world.* New York: Fordham University Press.

Broeze, F. (2002). *The globalization of the oceans: containerization from the 1950s to the present.* St. John's, NL: International Maritime Economic History Association.

Griscom, A. (2006). G.E.'s green gamble. *Vanity Fair,* VF.COM, 10 July.

Frock, R. (2006). *Changing how the world does business: FedEx's incredible journey to success—the inside story.* San Francisco: Berrett-Koehler.

Levinson, M. (2006). *The box, how the shipping container made the world smaller and the world economy bigger.* Princeton, NJ: Princeton University Press.

Truth 48

Rogers, E. (2006). *Diffusion of innovations*, 5th edn. New York: Free Press.

Truth 49

Altshuller, G. (2002). *40 principles: TRIZ keys to technical innovation.* Worcester, MA: Technical Innovation Center, Inc.

Johansson, F. (2004). *The Medici effect: breakthrough insights at the intersection of ideas, concepts, and cultures.* Boston, MA: Harvard Business School Press.

Truth 50

Howe, M.J., Davidson, J.W. & Sluboda, J.A. (1998). Innate talents: reality or myth? Behavioral and Brain Sciences, Vol. 21, No. 3, pp. 399–407.

McGraw, T.K. (2007). *Prophet of innovation: Joseph Schumpeter and creative destruction.* Boston, MA: The Belknap Press of Harvard University Press.

Norbert, M.J. (2006). The impact of digital file sharing on the music industry: an empirical analysis. *Topics in Economic Analysis & Policy*, Vol. 6, Issue 1, Article 18.

Schumpeter, J. (1912/1934). *The theory of economic development: an enquiry into profits, capital, credit, interest, and the business cycle.* Boston, MA, Harvard University Press.

Schumpeter, J. (1942). *Capitalism, socialism, and democracy.* Boston, MA: Harvard University Press.

Smith, A. (1776). *The wealth of nations.* London: Everyman's Library (1991 edn).

Van De Ven, A., Polley, D.E., Raghu, G. & Venkatraman, S. (1999). *The innovation journey.* New York: Oxford University Press.

Truth 51

Van De Ven, A.H. & Poole, M.S. (eds.), (2004). *Handbook of organizational change and innovation.* Oxford: Oxford University Press.

Truth 52

Gelb, M. & Miller-Caldicott, S. (2007). *Innovate like Edison: the success system of America's greatest inventor.* New York: Dutton.

Gemünden, H.G., Salomo, S. & Hölzle, K. (2007). Role models for radical innovations in times of open innovation. *Creativity and Innovation Management,* 16 (4), pp. 408–421.

Haikio, M. (2002). *Nokia: the inside story.* Harlow: FT Prentice Hall.

Hargadon, A. & Sutton, R. (2001). Building an innovation factory. *Harvard Business Review,* (Feb), pp. 157–166.

Kiley, D. (2004). *Driven—inside BMW, the most admired car company in the world.* Hoboken, NJ: John Wiley & Sons.

Xu, F. & Rickards, T. (2007). Creative management: a predicted development from research into creativity and management. *Creativity and Innovation Management,* Vol. 16, No. 3, pp. 216–228.

Truth 53

Baird, R.R. (2001). Experts sometimes show more false recall than novices: a cost of knowing too much. *Learning and Individual Differences,* Vol. 13, Issue 4, pp. 349–355.

Cerf, C. & Navasky, V. (1984). *The experts speak: the definitive compendium of authoritative misinformation.* New York: Pantheon Books.

Eichenwald, K. (2005). *Conspiracy of fools: a true story.* New York: Broadway Books.

Halberstam, D. (1993). *The best and the brightest.* New York: Fawcett Books; Twentieth-anniversary edition.

Horibe, F. (2001). *Creating the innovation culture: leveraging visionaries, dissenters, and other useful troublemakers in your organization.* Hoboken, NJ: John Wiley & Sons.

Leonard, D. & Swap, W. (2005). Deep smarts: how to cultivate and transfer enduring business wisdom. Boston, MA: Harvard Business School Press.

Rabe, C.B. (2006). *Innovation killers: how what we know limits what we can imagine—and what smart companies are doing about it.* New York: American Management Association.

Sackett, D.L. (2000). Personal views: the sins of expertness and a proposal for redemption. *British Medical Journal*, 6 May, 320(7244), p. 1283.

Truth 54

Masters, C. (2007). How Boeing got going. *Time Magazine*, 17 September.

Nelson, D., Mayo, R. & Moody, P.E. (1998). *Powered by Honda: developing excellence in the global enterprise.* Hoboken, NJ: John Wiley & Sons.

Seely-Brown, J. & Hagel, J. (2005). Innovation blowback: disruptive management practices from Asia. *The McKinsey Quarterly*, No. 1.

Truth 55

Burgelman, R. & Grove, A. (2001). *Strategy is destiny: how strategy-making shapes a company's future.* New York: Free Press.

Christensen, C.M., Anthony, S.D. & Roth, E.A. (2004). *Seeing what's next.* Boston, MA: Harvard Business School Press.

Pascale, R., Milleman, M. & Gioja, L. (2000). *Surfing the edge of chaos: the laws of nature and the new laws of business.* New York: Crown Business.

Readers Digest (1978). *The world's last mysteries.* London: Readers Digest Association.

Acknowledgements

Throughout the creation of this book, many people were kind enough and smart enough to share useful ideas and send valuable feedback.

In the tradition of the movies, hackers, and computer games, here is the roll call of many of the great and the good:

Tom Van den Eynde, Greg Bruce, Ellen DiResta, Ray Miller, Hannes Helander, Barry Brooks, Lawrence Lerner, Rajat Saigal, Dan Lucarelli, Rahim Dawood, Ranjit Sodhi, Saverio Baggio, Mark Cetnar, Cathy Cowin, Terrence Seamon, Raymond Miller, Steve Metcalfe, Larry MacDonald, Michael Scott, Paul Williams, Simon Cooper, Eric Cohen, Francois Andlau, Laurent Uhres, Gary Pine, Alexander Arendar, Johannes Schwaninger, David Atkinson, Philippe Gosseye, Olivier Van Duüren, Ludo H. Vandervelden, Richard Stagg, Mark Garland, Jon Pincus, Donna Fontaine, Mikel Lewis, Jonathan Schneider, Jan-Henrik Andersson, Raja Sekhar Malapati, Tamara Pesick, Kelly Amsbry, Garf Collins, Hannah Underwood and her second baby, Michael Aday, Jamen Shively, Robin Ruikers, Steve Swann, Adam Milligan, Steve Fortune, Samantha Jackson, Mike Steep, Maxine Horn, Jeffery Phillips, Graham Cook, Jost Wahlen, Roberto Carlos Mayer, Steve Hartley, Nadeem Shabir, Leatham Green, Anish Padinjaroote, Bruce Yang, David Pearlstein, Avis Austin, Laura Blake, Nancy Cronin, Matt Tognetti, Hamish Taylor, George Lamptey, Tom Jollands, Richard Elmes, Alex Freeburne, Reut Schwartz-Hebron, Matt Miller, Hauke Schupp, Sudershan Banerjee, Jack Walser, Buckley Brinkman, Debra Forman, John Zawacki, Kavita Khanna, Gregory Miller, Vikram Khanna, Bhanu Potta, Arash Dowlatshahi, Lomesh Dutta, Shahzad Masud, Mark Atkinson, Chris Scott, Steve Sutton, Steve Law, Michael Chevalier, Anish Padinjaroote, Han Koopmans, Navneet Bhushan, Gregory Watson, Jan de Liefde, Kirill Zlotnikov, David Crozier, Sean Mileusnic, Holly Rick, Jacob Kaldenbaugh, Subbarao Jayanti, Gianluca Corazza, Svend Haugaard, Andrei Titov, Adrian S. Petrescu, Barbara Simms Hudock, Christopher Montaño, Matthew Anderson, Paul S. Nowak, Bert Zethof, Carol Long, Raj Shankar, John Craig, Alexandre Marcondes, Jim Todhunter, Robert Gould, Ola Odumosu, Philippa Hird, Tom McMail, and Piero Beltrame.

About the author

Max Mckeown is a new breed of management guru. Brilliant, young, original and entertaining, he could become the most listened-to British business thinker of the new era. Max works as a strategy and innovation coach for the most admired companies in the world. He is also a sought-after speaker on subjects including innovation, engagement, human potential, customer experience, marketing, team building and competitive advantage.

He has been elected to the Customer Service Hall of Fame, been nominated as a Star of Human Resources by Personnel Today, is a Fellow of the RSA, and been featured on national and international radio, television and newspapers. Max has written seven books, including *E-Customer*, an insight into evolving customer behaviour; *Why They Don't Buy*, an end-to-end guide to building profitable customer relationships across multiple channels; and *Unshrink*, featuring the myths that stop people doing their best work and a set of new principles to engage their interest and ability. He conducts his research in collaboration with Warwick Business School. He can be reached at max@maxmckeown.com and through his website at www.maxmckeown.com

THE TRUTH ABOUT

THE TRUTH ABOUT **HIRING THE BEST** "Get the best and avoid the rest..." CATHY FYOCK	**THE TRUTH** ABOUT **MANAGING PEOPLE** "You get out of it what you put into it" STEPHEN P ROBBINS	**THE TRUTH** ABOUT **NEGOTIATIONS** "You may want to make the first offer" LEIGH L THOMPSON	**THE TRUTH** ABOUT **GETTING THE BEST FROM PEOPLE** "You get the best by giving the best..." MARTHA I. FINNEY
THE TRUTH ABOUT **CONFIDENT PRESENTING** "Focus on what can go right and win them over" JAMES O'ROURKE	**THE TRUTH** ABOUT **MAKING SMART DECISIONS** "Improve every single decision you make, starting right now..." ROBERT E. GUNTHER	**THE TRUTH** ABOUT **MANAGING CHANGE** "Life is 10% of what happens to you and 90% of how you react" WILLIAM KANE	**THE TRUTH** ABOUT **INNOVATION** "A small book about big ideas" MAX McKEOWN
THE TRUTH ABOUT **MANAGING BRANDS** "Marketing is courtship, not combat..." BRIAN TILL & DONNA HECKLAR	**THE TRUTH** ABOUT **GETTING THINGS DONE** "You need to believe it in order to achieve it..." MARK FRITZ	**THE TRUTH** ABOUT **EMAIL MARKETING** "Length does matter" G. SIMMS JENKINS	

9780273715337 · 9780273715320 · 9780273715313 · 9780273718086 · 9780273718079 · 9780273718062 · 9780273718291 · 9780273719120 · 9780273740751 · 9780273718390 · 9780273722298